History of Anthropology

History of Anthropology

By
ALFRED C. HADDON
M.A., Sc.D., F.R.S., Fellow of Christ's College, Cambridge; formerly
University Reader in Ethnology, Cambridge

With an Introduction by
Dr. Sumahan Bandyopadhyay
Assistant Professor, Department of Anthropology
Vidyasagar University
Medinipur (WB)

CONCEPT PUBLISHING COMPANY PVT. LTD.
NEW DELHI-110059

ISBN-13: 978-93-5125-263-4 (HB)
ISBN-13: 978-93-5125-264-1 (PB)

With New Introduction 2017

Published and Printed by

Concept Publishing Company Pvt. Ltd.
Regd. Office:
A/15-16, Commercial Block, Mohan Garden,
New Delhi-110059 (INDIA)
Phones : 25351460, 25351794, *Fax* : 091-11-25357109
Email : publishing@conceptpub.com
Website: www.conceptpub.com

Editorial Office: H-13, Bali Nagar, New Delhi-110 015, India.

Cataloging in Publication Data--Courtesy: D.K. Agencies (P) Ltd. <docinfo@dkagencies.com>

Haddon, Alfred C. (Alfred Cort), 1855-1940, **author.**
History of anthropology / by Alfred C. Haddon ; with an introduction by Dr. Sumahan Bandyopadhyay.
pages cm
Reprint with a new introduction. Second published: 1934.
Includes bibliographical references and index.
ISBN 9789351252641 (PB)
ISBN 9789351252634 (HB)

1. Anthropology--History. I. Title.

GN17.H33 2017 DDC 301.09 23

Preface

When it was suggested that I should bring out a second edition of *The History of Anthropology* I soon found that it was possible to retain only relatively small portions of the first edition, in which I was so ably helped by Mrs. A. Hingston Quiggin. There is indeed so much new matter that this is virtually a new book.

A book of such small size which deals with so vast a subject, comprising so many different studies, cannot satisfy the specialists in the several departments. Mention has been made only of some of those whose work notably contributed to or illustrates the growth of Anthropology. Doubtless many will criticize the amount of space allocated to certain authors, and wonder why others have been omitted or have received, but scanty recognition. "Meddling with questions of merit or priority is a thorny business at the best of times," as Huxley remarked. All I can say in extenuation for the selection is that the task has been by no means an easy one, and that I have been guided in some degree by the fact that the readers will mainly be of British nationality.

In most cases references are given in the text; a few works are listed at the ends of the several sections, but all these must not be taken in any sense as a bibliography, though students will find in the books cited all the necessary references to other literature. The two dates which follow a name refer to the years of the individual's birth and death; a single date refers to the date of publication of the book or memoir.

It may be objected that insufficient attention has been given to labourers in the field and perhaps too much to armchair workers, but this is necessitated by the compass of the book. Detailed investigations, however valuable and interesting, are after all, but material to be merged into generalizations, and generalizations proceed mainly from armchairs.

Professor Michael Foster somewhere remarked that "hypothesis is the salt of science." Observers in the field have to rely upon what they can see for themselves or be told by their informants. When an investigator has left his field and is working up his results at home he only too frequently finds that he has omitted to inquire about certain customs or beliefs which might reasonably be expected to occur there. This is the justification for questionaires. It is one of the most important functions of stay-at-home synthetic students laboriously to cull data from the vast literature of anthropology, travel, and ancient and modern history, and to weld them into coherent hypotheses. The student at home in this way suggests fresh inquiries to the field anthropologist, and a richer harvest is the result. The most valuable generalizations are made, however, when the observer is at the same time a generalizer; but "doubtless" as Maharbal said to Hannibal after the battle of Cannae, "the gods have not bestowed everything on the same man. You, Hannibal, know how to conquer; but you do not know how to use your victory."

The following scheme indicates the scope of Anthropology—

Human Biology

Physical Anthropology (Anthropology of some writers): The anatomy of man so far as it serves to distinguish (1) man from the apes, or (2) the living and extinct varieties of mankind. The evolution of man. Thus, it has zoological and palaeontological aspects.

The comparative study of the bodily functions (Comparative Physiology, including hormones and blood-groups) and of mental processes (Comparative Psychology).

The races of man and their distribution.

Racial mixture. The influence of the environment on physique. Human heredity and genetics. Eugenics.

Cultural Anthropology (Ethnology of some writers)

The comparative study of languages (Linguistics).

The arts and crafts (Technology) and their distribution and diffusion in space and time (Archaeology). The grouping of artifacts into complexes and the diffusion of these complexes.

The comparative study and classification of peoples based on their material and social cultures. The influence of environment on culture. Social psychology. The migrations and diffusions of cultures. The survival of early conditions in later times (Folklore).

The description of the structure and function of individual and group elements in social culture and of the cultures themselves; the classification of cultures; the social changes that take place in cultures and their psychological significance (Comparative Sociology). Social and religious groupings. Government and laws. Moral ideas. Magical and religious ideas and practices.

Ethnography

The intensive study and description of a particular group or area dealing with all of the above.

Contents

List of Figures

Introduction

The name of Alfred Cort Haddon is popularly known to the anthropology world in connection with his association in the team of Torres Straits Expedition in 1898. He was one of the builders of anthropology in Great Britain and contributed substantially to the professionalization of the discipline. Torres Straits expedition has been called the first anthropological field exercise (Eriksen, 2001). Haddon's role in this expedition was pivotal. In the division of labour as planned for this collective field enterprise, Haddon was to collect data on ethnology and folklore.

Apart from his pioneering role in field studies in anthropology, he must be remembered for another reason that is his small book: *History of Anthropology.* After its first publication in 1910, he brought out the book for the second time in 1934 as a part of the Thinker's Library Series Publication (No. 42). The series had the reputation for printing some of the epoch making publications such as *A Short History of the World* by H.G. Wells, *On Liberty* by John Stuart Mill, *The Origin of Species* and *Descent of Man* by Charles Darwin, Anthropology by E.B. Tylor etc.

Haddon was born on 24 May, 1855 in London. He got his B.A. from University of Cambridge in 1878. He obtained Sc.D. from the same university in 1897. In professional life, he started his career as a marine biologist. He was a Professor of Zoology in Royal College of Science in Dublin (Vered, 2004). Ten years ahead of his celebrated anthropological expedition to Torres Straits, he had been to the same place to study the marine biological life. But he was drawn much to the life of the islanders and he was struck by the fear that their culture would soon vanish under the European influence. He began to collect data on the life of these people from different regions. He conducted fieldwork in the coastal Ireland. In 1893, he did ethnographic study on the Aran Islanders. Thus his Torres Strait expedition was preceded by a number of expeditions of ethnographic nature.

In 1901, Haddon joined University of Cambridge as Lecturer in Ethnology. At this stage Sir James George Frazer influenced him a lot. Haddon visited United States. There he came under the influence of Franz Boas. This interaction prompted him to introduce a curriculum in Cambridge following the Columbia University's course of study. A post-graduate programme of study was started in 1906 in Cambridge. The undergraduate studies in that university had its beginning in 1913. He stressed the need of fieldwork in anthropology. However, he did not undermine the importance of generalizations by decrying armchair anthropology. He wrote:

> "Detailed investigations, however valuable and interesting, are after all but material to be merged into generalizations, and generalizations proceed mainly from armchairs."
>
> (Haddon, 1934:vi)

This understanding was fundamental to the formulation of the methodology for the newly introduced discipline of anthropology.

Haddon's *History of Anthropology* (1910) has been the first effort of this kind to give an outline of the development in the discipline up to that period. The 1934 edition, which has been followed here was completely revised by Haddon. For Haddon, the scope of anthropology is spread in three major subdivisions: Human Biology, Cultural Anthropology (Ethnology) and Ethnography. He made a difference between ethnology and ethnography. Ethnography is the intensive study and description of a particular group or area dealing with language, technology, arts and crafts, material and social life (he called 'social cultures'), influence of environment, folklore, law, religion, structure and function of group elements. All these aspects studied in ethnography with reference to a particular group constitute the subject matter of anthropology. In fact he mentioned that cultural anthropology is also termed as ethnology by some writers. This understanding of ethnography and ethnology still holds ground to certain extent as the description of a particular culture is ethnography and their comparative study is ethnology.

History of Anthropology has three main sections which are again distributed into altogether nine chapters. Three major divisions are—Human Biology, Cultural Anthropology or Ethnology and Comparative Sociology. Unlike the approaches to study the historical development of anthropology by focusing on the contribution of individual anthropologist (Lowie, 1937; Kuper, 1983; Moore, 2011), or periodical developments (Penniman, 1974; Originally published in 1935), or theoretical developments (Barnard, 2000; Layton, 1997; Harris, 2001), Haddon tried to narrate the development of different branches of knowledge in anthropology. Authors like Hatch (1973), Stocking (1995), Eriksen and Nielsen (2001) have given emphasis both on the scholar as well as the theoretical schools that developed side by side. Darnell (1974) narrates the development in American anthropology under four sections in her book. The sections or parts deal with nature and definition of anthropology, voyagers and philosophers, professionalization and history from within the discipline. Since 1980s the writing of history of anthropology began to take up novel ways to look at the past anthropological development. Kardiner and Preble (1961) focused on the individual scholars who made substantial contribution in the study of man. In their book we find life sketches of Darwin, Spencer, Tylor, Frazer, Durkheim, Boas, Malinowski, Kroeber, Benedict and Freud. We come across a book exclusively on Franz Boas written by Stocking. In the volume edited by Vermeulen and Rolden (1995) essays on origin, contributions by individual anthropologists, national traditions in European countries have been compiled within two covers. Layton (1997) intended to provide a complete history of anthropological thought. The book dealt with the idea of social system, functionalism, structuralism, interactionist theories, Marxist anthropology, socio-ecology and post-modernism. Barnard (2000) stated that his goal was to present the development of anthropological ideas against a background of the converging and diverging interests of its practitioners. In Moore's (2011) book there are six parts dealing with founders, culture, society, evolution, adaptation and materialist theories, structures, symbol and meaning, practice, agency, power. Moore discussed the life and works of scholars who contributed most prominently under each section. In India, we find several efforts that bear influence of both Penniman (*ibid.*) as well as Haddon (Majumdar, 1950; Bose, 1963; Vidyarthi, 1978; Danda, 1988; Joardar, 2001).

For the first time, Haddon pointed out that the roots of anthropology should be traced into the writings of Greek scholars like Herodotus, Aristotle, Lucretius, Strabo and others. In the present day publications, these scholars are being studied for anthropological references in their works (Eriksen and Nielsen, 2001; Launey, 2010). Launey (2010) has edited a volume on the history of anthropology. He compiled the writings of the scholars who wrote on other cultures or provided significant anthropological resources. His book starts with the writing of Herodotus. However, it is strange that none of the above two books referred to Haddon's book that possesses the seminal contribution. Haddon's work is significant for many other reasons. In his we find the discussion on the influence of environment on culture. It was much before the days of cultural ecology advocated by Julian Steward. He did not forget to write about the history of archaeological discoveries. He arranged the information available so far on the lithic cultural periods and regional traditions like Abbevillian, Mousterian etc. Therefore, it can be said that in his book he has discussed about all the four major branches of anthropology (called Four Field Approach today).

We often got engaged into a debate what should be the appropriate nomenclature for one of the major divisions of anthropology called cultural anthropology by some, social anthropology by others and is also known as social-cultural anthropology. The term social anthropology is said to be preferred in England whereas cultural anthropology has its adherence in United States. However, we find that Haddon used the term cultural anthropology in his book. Does it indicate the American influence on anthropology in Britain in the beginning?

This celebrated and pioneering work of anthropology is being published for greater readership of the present generations to keep them abreast of the very foundational ideas in the discipline of anthropology. The book brings before us many of the informations that prove useful even today.

Shri A.K. Mittal of Concept Publishing Co. (P.) Ltd. deserves special acknowledgement for coming forward to print this book with due care and regard for its worthiness in the History of Anthropology.

15 April, 2016

Dr. Sumahan Bandyopadhyay
Department of Anthropology
Vidyasagar University
Rangamati, Medinipur - 721102
West Bengal

References

Amit, Vered, (Ed.) 2004. *Biographical Dictionary of Social and Cultural Anthropology.* Routledge. London.

Barnard, Alan, 2000. *History and Theory in Anthropology.* Cambridge University Press. Cambridge.

Bose, N.K., 1963. *Fifty Years of Science in India – Progress of Anthropology and Archaeology.* Indian Science Congress Association. Calcutta.

Danda, Ajit K. 1988. Development of Anthropology: The Indian Perspectives. *Journal of the Indian Anthropological Society.* 23(2): 141-155.

Darnell, Regna 1974. *Readings in the History of Anthropology.* Harper and Row. New York.

Eriksen, Thomas, Hylland and Finn Sivert Nielsen, 2001. *A History of Anthropology.* Pluto Press. London.

Haddon, A.C. 1934. *History of Anthropology.* Watts & Co., London.

Harris, Marvin 2001. *The Rise of Anthropological Theory.* Altamira Press. London.

Hatch, Elvin 1973. *Theories of Man and Culture.* Columbia University Press. New York.

Joardar, B. 2001. *Anthropology in the Making: The Indian Experience.* Inter-India Publications. New Delhi.

Kardiner, Abram and Edward Preble, 1963. *They Studied Man.* Mentor Books. New York.

Kuklick, Henrika, 1991. *The Savage Within: The Social History of British Anthropology, 1885-1945.* Cambridge University Press. Cambridge.

_______ (Ed.) 2008. *A New History of Anthropology.* Blackwell Publishers. Malden. Mass.

Kuper, Adam, 1983. *Anthropology and Anthropologists.* Routledge and Kegan Paul. London.

Launay, Robert, (Ed.) 2010. *Foundations of Anthropological Theory.* Wiley-Blackwell. Malden.

Layton, Robert, 1997. *An Introduction to Theory in Anthropology.* Cambridge University Press. Cambridge.

Lowie, Robert H. 1937. *The History of Ethnological Theory.* Farrar & Reinhart, Inc. New York.

Majumdar, D.N., 1950. Anthropology under Glass. *Journal of Anthropological Society of Bombay.* Special Issue 1-16.

Moore, Jerry D. 2011. *An Introduction to Anthropological Theories and Theorists.* Rawat Publications. Jaipur.

Patterson, Thomas C. 2001. *A Social History of Anthropology in the United States.* Berg Publishers. New York.

Penniman, T.K. 1974 (1935) A Hundred Years of Anthropology. William Morrow & Co., Inc. New York.

Stocking Jr. George W. (Ed.) 1974. *The Shaping of American Anthropology, 1883-1911: A Franz Boas Reader.* Basic Books. New York.

Stocking Jr. George W. 1983-1989. *History of Anthropology.* Five Volumes. University of Wisconsin Press. Madison.

——1995. *After Tylor—British Social Anthropology 1881-1951.* Athlone. London.

Uberoi, Patricia, Nandini Sundar, and Satish Deshpande, 2007. *Anthropology in the East.* Permanent Black. Ranikhet.

Vermeulen Han F. and Arturo Alvarez Rold[illegible] 1995. *Fieldwork and Footnotes: Studies in the History of European Anthropology.* Routledge. London.

Vidyarthi, L.P. 1978. *Rise of Anthropology in India: A Social Science Orientation.* Vols. I & II. Concept Publishing Company Pvt. Ltd., New Delhi

E.B. Tylor

Chapter I
The Pioneers of Physical Anthropology

Aristotle, "the father of them that know," as Dante called him, is credited with having coined the word "anthropologist"; but he did not employ it in a very complimentary sense. Describing a lofty-minded man in his *Ethics,* he terms him οὐχ ανθρωπολογος—not a gossip, not a talker about himself. But the word does not seem to have supplied a permanent want in the Greek world, and we next meet it in a Latin form in the sixteenth century. *Anthropologium* was then used in a restricted sense, relating to man's bodily structure; and the first work in which it occurs is generally stated to be Magnus Hundt's *Anthropologium de hominis dignitate,* which appeared in 1501, and dealt in a general way with human anatomy and physiology.

The first appearance of the word in English was probably in the seventeenth century, when an anonymous book was published bearing the title *Anthropologie abstracted; or, the idea of Humane nature reflected in briefe Philosophicall and anatomical collections* (1655). The author defines his subject thus:—

> Anthropologie, or the history of human nature, is, in the vulgar (yet just) impression, distinguished into two volumes: the first entitled *Psychologie,* the nature of the rational soule discoursed; the other anatomie, or the fabrick or structure of the body of man revealed in dissection... of the former we shall in a distracted rehersall, deliver our collections.[1]

The meaning of the word was scarcely clear in the beginning of the nineteenth century, when we find, in the *British Encyclopedia* of 1822, the following definitions: "A discourse upon human nature," and "among Divines that manner of expression by which the inspired writers attribute human parts and passions to God."

Concerning the present use of the term "Anthropology," few will take exception to the definition given by Topinard in his *l'Anthropologie* (1876): "Anthropology is the branch of natural history which treats of man and the races of man." It may be yet more succinctly described as "the science of man," which comprises two main divisions—the one which deals with the natural man (ἄνθρωπος, or *homo*); the other which is concerned with man in relation to his fellows, or in other words with social man (ἔθνος, or *socius).* The classification here adopted is given at the end of the Preface. It should, however, be stated that, whereas in this country we employ the term "Anthropology" to cover the whole subject, it is common on the Continent to restrict the term to what we designate as "Physical Anthropology".

When men consider themselves in relation to others two sentiments are present: "Consciousness of kind," as F.H. Giddings termed it *(The Principles of Sociology,* 1896), which was recognized by W. McDougall as derived from the "gregarious impulse". He says: "In any human being the instinct operates most powerfully in relation to, and receives the highest degree of satisfaction from the presence of, the human beings who most closely resemble that individual, those who behave in like manner and respond to the same situations with similar emotions."[2] Conversely this implies the recognition of unlikeness, or race discrimination.

Ancient literature and the pictorial art of certain uncivilized peoples abound in examples of race discrimination. The crude representations of human beings discovered in caves in France and elsewhere were doubtless intended to portray the people themselves who lived in the Upper Palaeolithic period. These

Fig. 1.1: Bushmen Raiding Kafir Cattle (After R. Andree)

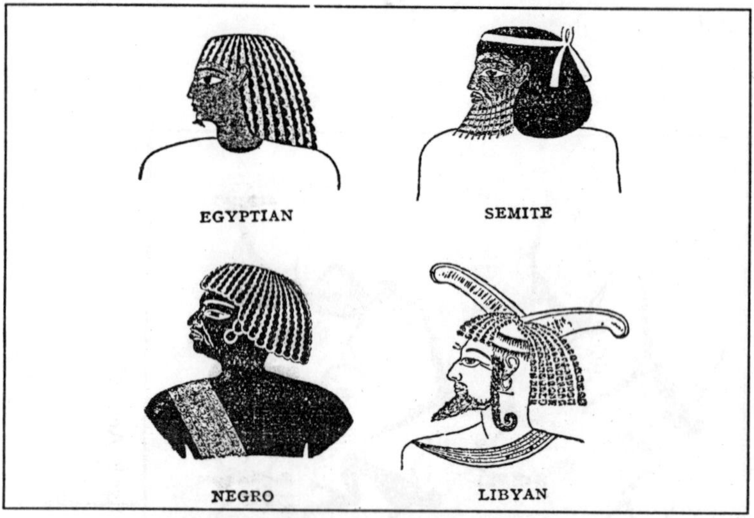

Fig. 1.2: Ancient Egyptian Race Portraiture
Tombs of the Kings at Binan-el-Molouk (XVIIIth-XXIst Dynasties)

drawings or carvings, like those of most modern savages, exhibit much greater skill in delineating animals than human beings; consequently, it is dangerous to rely on them as representing the physical characteristics of the then existing populations. Very different is the famous Bushman pictograph of a fight between Bushmen and Kafirs. Here relative size, the difference in colour, and the employment of different implements of war by these two races are strikingly exemplified; but as a general rule the Bushmen themselves exaggerate certain features and minimize others—for example, the head is invariably too small and featureless.

In Egypt there is an immense amount of pictorial and sculptured material for ethnological study, covering a range of many centuries. Over three thousand years ago the artists—"untrained but not unobservant ethnologists"[3]—decorated the walls of royal tombs with representations of the four races of mankind, among whom the Egyptians of the nineteenth dynasty supposed the world to be partitioned—(1) The Egyptians, whom they painted red; (2) the Asiatics or Semites, yellow; (3) the Southerns or Negroes, black;

and (4) the Libyans, Westerners or Northerners, white, with blue eyes and fair beards. Each type is clearly differentiated by peculiar dress and characteristic features. In addition to these four types, other human varieties were delineated by the Ancient Egyptians, most of which can be identified. "On the Egyptian monuments, however, we not only find very typical portraits, but also an attempt at classification, for the Egyptians were a scientific people with a knowledge of medicine, and also skilled mathematicians; therefore, their primitive anthropology is not unexpected."[4] This facility for race discrimination was still earlier exhibited in the prehistoric or early historic slate palettes of Egypt.

Belonging to the fifth century B.C. are the realistic portraiture figurines in pottery discovered by Professor Flinders Petrie[5] at Memphis, "which clearly are copied from various races which were welded together by the Persians, and who all met in the foreign settlement in Memphis." He identifies Sumerians or Accadians, the old Turanian people who started civilization in Babylonia. "Their heads are identified by closely similar portraits carved in stone about 3000 B.C., and found in Mesopotamia." Parisians, Scythians, Mongols, and even Indians, are also recognizable; but some of the latter are dated by him at about 200 B.C.

Assyrian monuments are less explicit in this respect.

> The Assyrians themselves are shown to have been of a very pure type of Semites, but in the Babylonians there is a sign of Cushite blood.... There is one portrait of an Elamite (Cushite) king on a vase found at Susa; he is painted black and thus belongs to the Cushite race. The Ethiopian type can be clearly seen in the reliefs depicting the Assyrian wars with the kings of Ethiopia, but it is hard to discriminate Arabs or Jews from Assyrians; in fact it is only in the time of good art that distinctions are traceable.[6]

Rock carvings in Persia, Scythian coins, and numerous other monuments and remains from other countries and belonging to diverse ages, illustrate that the head-form, features, character of the hair and mode of wearing it, ornaments, dress, and weapons, were all recognized as means of discriminating between different peoples from the earliest times.

Ancient literature, of which one example must suffice, tells the same tale:

> The sense of differences of colour, which, for all our talk of common humanity, still plays a great, and, politically, often an inconvenient, part in the history of the world, finds forcible expression in the Vedic descriptions of the people whom the Aryans found in possession of the plains of India. In a well-known passage the god Indra is praised for having protected the Aryan colour, and the word meaning colour *(varna)* is used down to the present day as the equivalent of caste, more especially with reference to the castes believed to be of Aryan descent.[7]

The word "caste" is of Portuguese origin. In the 179th hymn of the first Mandala of the Rig-Veda, as Dr. Gerson da Cunha points out,[8] the word *varna* is used in the dual number, *ubhau varnau,* "two colours," white of the Aryans and black of the Dasyus—that is, of the "Dravidian" aborigines, who are elsewhere called "black-skinned," "unholy," "excommunicated". Other texts dwell on their low stature, coarse features, and their voracious appetite. The Rig-Veda employs the word *anâsa*—"noseless"—to characterize the Dasyus and Daityas, which designations mean "thieves" or "demons". It is hardly an exaggeration to say that from these sources there might be compiled a fairly accurate anthropological definition of the jungle tribes of today.

Thus were the foundations of descriptive anthropology unconsciously laid.

In our own day racial characters are seized upon in the same manner, and racial antipathy adds fuel to its own fire in regarding traits which differ from those of the speaker or writer as being ugly, objectionable, or of low type. "The study of race," said the late Sir William Flower (1831-1899), "is at a low ebb indeed when we hear the same contemptuous epithet of "nigger" applied indiscriminately by the Englishman abroad to the blacks of the West Coast of Africa, the Kaffirs of Natal, the Lascars of Bombay, the Hindoos of Calcutta, the aborigines of Australia, and even the Maories of New Zealand."[9] The Englishman who condemns as a "nigger" any dark-skinned native has not advanced in race discrimination beyond his remote kinsman who crossed into the valley of the Indus some four thousand years ago.

Hippocrates (460-377 B.C.), "the Father of Physic," was certainly a pioneer in physical anthropology. He says: "I will pass over the smaller differences among nations, but will now treat of such as are great either from nature or custom; and, first, concerning the macrocephali. There is no other race of men which have heads in the least resembling theirs." He believed that this elongated conformation of the head was originally produced artificially; but subsequently it was inherited, or, as he puts it: "Thus, at first usage operated, so that, this constitution was the result of force; but in the course of time it was formed naturally, so that, usage had nothing to do with it"—a view adopted many centuries later by Buffon and others.[10]

Aristotle may be described as the first anthropologist. Material had been collected by travellers, such as Hanno, the Carthaginian, who encountered gorillas in Africa; by historians, such as Herodotus (who was also a traveller); and by doctors, such as Hippocrates. Aristotle was indebted to some extent to all of these; but his vast works in natural history were based mainly on what he considered of primary importance—facts of actual personal knowledge derived from personal observation. On this account alone his writings deserved the place which they held for many centuries.

Thus, undisturbed by the dogmas of religion or philosophy, he placed man naturally among the animals (being thus, as Topinard remarks, about twenty centuries ahead of humanity), but distinguished from them by certain features—by the relative size of the brain, by two-leggedness, by mental characters etc. Some writers regard it as improbable that either Hippocrates or Aristotle had ever dissected the human body, but it is also possible to hold the opposite view.

Vesalius (1513-1564) is the next great name in the history of physical anthropology. He was Professor of Anatomy at Padua, Bologna, and Pisa, and physician to Charles V and Philip II. His work marks a revolution in anatomical science; for not only did he overthrow the doctrines which had been accepted for fourteen centuries, demonstrating that to a great extent Galen had studied the anatomy of the ape rather than that of man, but, by his own deductions from direct observation and original research, he established a fresh and unassailable foundation for future investigation. His fate was not unlike that of many other daring pioneers of the Middle Ages. He was accused of having dissected a man while yet alive, and was dragged by his enemies before the Inquisition and, condemned to death. By the intercession of the king his sentence was commuted into a pilgrimage to the Holy Sepulchre, but on his return journey he was shipwrecked and drowned off the island of Zante.

Cunningham[11] says:—

> It is interesting to note in passing that certain racial distinctions did not escape the eye of Vesalius. "It appears" he remarks, "that most nations have something peculiar in the shape of the head. The crania of the Genoese and, still more remarkable, those of the Greeks and Turks, are globular in form. This shape which they esteem elegant and well adapted to their practice of enveloping the head in the folds of their turbans, is often produced by the midwives at the solicitation of the mother." He further

> observes "that the Germans had generally a flattened occiput and broad head, because the children are always laid on their backs in the cradles; and that the Belgians have a more oblong form because the children are allowed to sleep on their sides."

We know that more or less continuous pressure is exerted on the pliable heads of infants to produce admired shapes, but the theory was carried rather too far when adduced, some centuries later, to account for the facial features of negroes. Lawrence in his *Lectures on Comparative Anatomy* (1844, p. 265) follows Blumenbach in attributing the flat noses and thick lips of the negro to the method of carrying babies in Africa. The negro mothers, while at work, carry their infants on their backs, and "in the violent motions required for their hard labour, as in beating or pounding millet etc., the face of the young one is said to be constantly thumping against the back of the mother." But, as Cunningham points out, no attempt was made to explain how the process of bumping produced exactly opposite results in the case of the nose and lips—reducing the prominence of the former and increasing the projection of the latter.[12] Even as late as 1923, J.L. Myres suggests that the physical characters of Mongoloid man may have been due to mode of life and to the infants drinking milk (as he supposes) directly from the udders of mares.[13]

"The invention of the 'lineae cephalometricae' of Spigel, who died in the early part of the seventeenth century, may perhaps be regarded as constituting the earliest scientific attempt at cranial measurement." He drew four lines in certain directions, and a skull in which these lines were equal to each other he regarded as regularly proportioned. "Although these lines are evidently not sufficient for the comparative ethnography of the present day, yet it is interesting to observe that, in ascending the zoological scale, these lines approximate equality just in proportion as the head measured approaches the human form."[14]

Johann Sperling, author of *Physica anthropologia* (1668), and Samuel Haworth, who wrote *Anthropologia; or A Philosophical Discourse Concerning Man* (1680), also belong to the seventeenth century. But more important is the work of Edward Tyson, a Cambridge man, who took his degree of Doctor of Medicine in 1678. His fame rests mainly on the work which laid the foundations of comparative morphology, *Orang-Outang, sive Homo Sylvestris: or, The Anatomy of a Pygmie compared with that of a Monkey, an Ape, and a Man* (1699). This was the first attempt to deal with the anatomy of any of the anthropoid apes, and shows very conspicuous ability on the part of the author. He compared the structure of man with that of the monkeys, and came to the conclusion that the pygmy formed a kind of intermediate animal between the two. The pygmy was, as a matter of fact, a chimpanzee, and its skeleton, which was thus early recognized as the "missing link," is still to be seen in the Natural History Museum (British Museum) at South Kensington. Tyson added to this work *A Philological Essay Concerning the Pygmies, the Cynocephali, the Satyrs, and Sphinges of the Ancients. Wherein it will appear that they are all either Apes or Monkeys, and not Men, as formerly pretended.*

This was the first attempt to explain in a rational fashion the innumerable tales found in all parts of the world about the existence of pygmy races, ape-men, or men-apes. Tyson's hypothesis was that all these legends were based on imperfect observations of apes, and he was followed by Buffon and others. It may be well here briefly to note the researches which have led in late years to the opposite conclusion—*i.e.* that the tales relate to a dwarf race of men formerly very widely spread over the globe.

This theory is mainly associated with the name of de Quatrefages. Analysing the evidence, he shows that the two localities where the ancients appear to place their pygmies (the interior of Africa and the southernmost parts of Asia), together with the characters assigned to them, indicate an actual knowledge of the two groups of small people (Negrilloes and Negritoes), who are still to be found in those regions. Professor J. Kollmann, of Basel, argues for the existence of a European pygmy race in Neolithic times from some remains found at Schaffhausen, and the wide prevalence of short statures among many peoples in Europe, especially in the south.[15] Dr. David Mac-Ritchie[16] attributes not only legends of pygmies, but fairy tales in general, to a prehistoric dwarf race. Dr. Windle sums up the question thus:—It is possible with more or less accuracy and certainty to identify most of those races which, described by the older. writers, had been rejected by their successors. Time has brought their revenge to Aristotle and Pliny by showing that they were right, where Tyson, and even Buff on, were wrong.[17]

In the time of Aristotle, Man took his place naturally at the head of the other animals, being distinguished from the brutes by certain characters. But the influence of religion and of philosophy did not long permit of this association. Man came to be regarded as the *chef d'oeuvre* of creation, a thing apart, a position aptly described in the words of Saint Paul (marginal version) "for a little while inferior to the angels."

In the eighteenth century came a startling change. Man was wrenched from this detached and isolated attitude, and linked on once more to the beasts of the field. This was the work of Linnaeus.

Linnaeus (1707-1778) was the son of a poor Swedish pastor, and his early life was a hard struggle. It was long before his work obtained recognition, but in 1757 by a patent of nobility he became Karl von Linné. Georges Louis Leclerc, Comte de Buffon (1707-1788), had wealthy parents and received a good education; but, although he lived a life of pleasure, he also was a hard worker, and in 1739 was appointed keeper of the Jardin du Roi and of the Royal Museum.

The genius of Linnaeus lay in classification. In his *Systema Naturoe* he fixed the place of Man in Nature, arranging *Homo sapiens* as a distinct species in the order Primates, and classified the varieties of man. This was abominable in the eyes of Buffon, who declared all classifications to be merely conventional. Buffon, as Topinard says, did not classify, he described; Cuvier had small opinion of the value of Buffon's work, while Camper and Saint Hilaire considered him the greatest naturalist of modern times. Linnaeus "found biology a chaos and left it a cosmos." Flourens said, "Previously man had only been studied as an individual, Buffon is the first who looked upon him as a species."[18] Buffon was no believer in the permanent stability of species; he hinted at a possible common ancestor for horse and ass, and for ape and man, but, since the Bible affirms to the contrary, "of course the thing cannot be."

It was fortunate for the nascent science that the next great name on its roll was that of a man of very wide reading, endowed with remarkable reasoning powers, and with exceptional perspicuity for sifting out the true from the false.

Professor Johann Friedrich Blumenbach of Göttingen (1752-1840) early turned his attention to the study of Man. He was the first to place anthropology on a rational basis, and in his *De generis humani varietate nativa* (1775-1795) laid the foundations of race classification based on measurement. He noted the variations in the shape of the skull and of the face, and to that extent may be regarded as the founder of craniology. There was a third field in which his work was equally valuable to his contemporaries.

Every successive age is astonished at the credulity of its predecessor; but when we remember the grave difficulties which beset the explorer even as late as the eighteenth century, and the wild "travellers' tales" which it was impossible either to verify or disprove, we can understand the credence given to the belief in "Anthropophagi, and men whose heads do grow beneath their shoulders." Tyson, in his *Philological Essay,* gives a list, chiefly derived from classical writers, of the "monstrous productions," belief in which had not altogether died out in the seventeenth century. Linnaeus did not include these in his *Homo Monstrosus;* but various questionable creatures are inserted by his pupil Hoppius in the treatise on the *Anthropomorpha* of Linnaeus, read in 1760.[19] Within the species *Homo sapiens* Linnaeus included wild or natural man, *Homo sapiens ferus,* whose existence was widely believed in at the time. The most authentic case was that of "Wild Peter," the naked brown boy discovered in 1724 in Hanover. He was sent to London, and under the charge of Dr. Arbuthnot became a noted personage and the subject of keen discussion among philosophers and naturalists. Blumenbach alone took the trouble to investigate the origin of Wild Peter, and finally proved that Peter was the dumb child of a widower, who had been thrust out of his home by a new step-mother.[20] Analogous cases of "wolf-man," and so forth, have since cropped up from time to time, but in every instance have been shown to be ordinary human beings who have run wild.

Notes

1. T. Bendyshe, "The History of Anthropology," *Mem. Anth. Soc.,* I, 1865, p. 356.
2. *An Introduction to Social Psychology*, 1908, p. 300.
3. D. Randall-Maciver and A. Wilkin, *Libyan Notes,* 1901, p. 1.
4. R.S. Poole, *Journ. Anth. Inst.,* XVI, 1887, p. 371; cf. also H. G. Tomkins, *J.A.I.* XVIII, 1889, p. 206, and W. M. Flinders Petrie, *ibid.,* XXXI, 1901, p. 248.
5. *Man,* VIII, 1908, p. 129.
6. Poole, *loc. cit.,* p. 371.
7. H.H. Risley, *The Tribes and Castes of Bengal: Ethnographic Glossary*, I, 1892, p. xxxviii.
8. "The Nasal Index in Biological Anthropology," *Journ. Anth. Soc. of Bombay,* 1892, p. 542.
9. *Report Brit. Assoc*., 1881, p. 683.
10. Adams, *Hippocrates. Sydenham Soc.*, I, p. 207.
11. *J.R.A.I.,* 1908, p. 15.
12. *l.c.,* p. 24.
13. *The Cambridge Ancient History*, I, p. 22.
14. J. Aitken Meigs, *North American Med.-Chir. Rev.,* 1861, p. 840.
15. "Das Schweizersbild bei Schaffhausen and Pygmaen in Europa," *Zeit. f. Ethnol*., XXVI, 1894, p.189.
16. *The Testimony of Tradition*, 1890; *Fians, dairies and Picts*, 1895.
17. *Essay concerning the Pygmies of the Ancients*, 1894, p. liii.

18. Topinard, *Élèments d'anth., gen.*, 1885, p. 48.
19. Bendyshe, *Mem. Anth. Soc., I,* 1865, pp. 430, 447.
20. *The Anthropological treatises of Johann Friedrich Blumenbach,* translated by T. Bendyshe for the Anthropological Society, 1865, p. 332.

Chapter II
The Systematization of Physical Anthropology

Hitherto we have been dealing with the great pioneers in Anthropology, those who laid the foundations, brought order out of chaos, and suggested the outlines of future work. Henceforward Anthropology may claim the name of a science, and the work developed on definite lines. It will be more convenient to treat the various branches separately, abandoning a strict chronological method.

The first branch to attract workers was Somatology, the physical aspect of man, of which we have already noted the inception. Not until the nineteenth century can Archaeology, or Prehistoric Anthropology, be said to have developed into a science; while the scientific study of Ethnology, or Cultural Anthropology, is barely half a century old.

Somatology had already been foreshadowed by Vesalius, Spigel, and Linnaeus; but Blumenbach was the first to strike its keynote by recording the shape of the skull and of the face. He was the fortunate possessor of a large number of skulls—large, that is, for his time—and he published a description of them (1790-1826), *Decas collectionis suae craniorum diversarum gentium illustrata,* with seventy plates. He noted particularly the *norma verticalis—i.e.* the shape of the skull as seen from above, distinguishing by its means three types—the square shape of the Mongols, the narrow or "pressed in from the sides" shape of the

Fig. 2.1: J.F. Blumenbach

Negroes, and the intermediate form which he recognized in the "Caucasians". He was the first to popularize craniology, and "its became the fashion to visit the Blumenbachian Museum, to have the differences which distinguish the different cranial types pointed out, and to indulge in sentimental rhapsodies upon the beauty and symmetry of the young female Georgian skull, which was considered to represent the highest type of all."[1] But Blumenbach does not seem to have taken advantage of his own discoveries. In choosing the *norma verticalis* as a racial criterion, he made a valuable contribution to science, but he did not reproduce his *normœ* in his plates, nor did he base his classification on them. Indeed, his typical Caucasian skull is really squarer than his typical Mongolian.

Peter Camper (1722-1789) had already been studying head-form, though from a totally different standpoint, and his deductions were not published until after his death. His contributions to anthropology were an essay *De l'Éducation physique des Enfans,* a lecture *De l'Origine et de la couleur des Nègres,* and a treatise *De l'Orang-outang, et de quelques autres espèces de Singes*; but only his work on the facial angle has attained permanent fame. His early inclinations were towards art, and it was in the interests of art, not of anthropology, that the researches that resulted in his determination of the facial angle came to be undertaken. He found that most artists painted Negroes with the faces of Europeans. To obtain the necessary facial effects distinguishing the Negro from the European, Camper devised his system of measurements. He drew a line from the aperture of the ear to the base of the nose, and another from the line of the junction of the lips (or, in the case of a skull, from the front of the incisor teeth) to the most prominent part of the forehead. "If," he said, "the projecting part of the forehead be made to exceed the 100th degree, the head becomes mis-shapen and assumes the appearance of hydrocephalus or watery head. It is very surprising that the artists of Ancient Greece should have chosen precisely the maximum, while the best Roman artists have limited themselves to the 95th degree, which is not so pleasing. The angle which the facial or characteristic line of the face makes," he continued, "varies from 70 to 80 degrees in the human species. All above is resolved by the rules of art; all below bears resemblance to that of apes. If I make the facial line lean forward, I have an antique head; if backward, the head of a Negro. If I still more incline it, I have the head of an ape; and if more still, that of a dog, and then that of an idiot."

Camper's facial angle may be of service to Art, but since the points from which the lines are drawn are all variable, owing to the disturbing influence of other factors, such as an increased length of face, or an unusually prominent brow-ridge, it cannot form an accurate measurement for Anthropology. It was severely criticized by Blumenbach, Lawrence, and Prichard, but adopted in France, and by Morton in America.

Dr. J. Aitken Meigs[2] pointed out that as early as 1553 the measurement of the head appears to have exercised the ingenuity of Albrecht Dürer, who, in his *De Symmetricâ Partium in Rectis Formis Humanorum Corporum,* has given such measurements in almost every view. These, however, are more artistic in their tendency and scope than scientific. A glance at some of the outline drawings of Dürer shows incontestable that the facial line and angle were not wholly unknown to him, and that Camper had rather elaborated than invented this method of cranial measurement. The artist seems to have entertained more philosophical views of cephalometry, or head measurement, than the professor.

The evolution of craniometrical measurements is of interest to the physical anthropologist, but even a brief recital of this progress would weary the non-specialist. A history of Anthropology, however, would not be complete if it ignored the general trend of such investigations.

Some of the early workers, such as Daubenton (1716-1799) and Mulder, Walther (1802), Barclay, and Serres (1857) in the first half of the nineteenth century, attempted to express the relation between the brain-case, and the face by some simple measurement or method of comparison in their endeavour to formulate not only the differences between the races of mankind, but also those which obtain between men and the lower animals.

Others during the same period investigated the relations and proportions of portions of the skull to the whole by means of lines. Spix[3] adopted five lines. J.G. von Herder[4] employed a series of lines radiating from the atlas (the uppermost bone of the vertebral column); but, more generally, the *meatus auditorius* (ear-hole) was the starting-point.[5]

The internal capacity of the skull first received attention from F. Tiedemann, who determined it by filling the skull with millet seed and then ascertaining the weight of the seed.[6] Morton first used white pepper seed, which he discarded later for No. 8 shot, while S. de Volkoff[7] employed water. Modifications in the use of

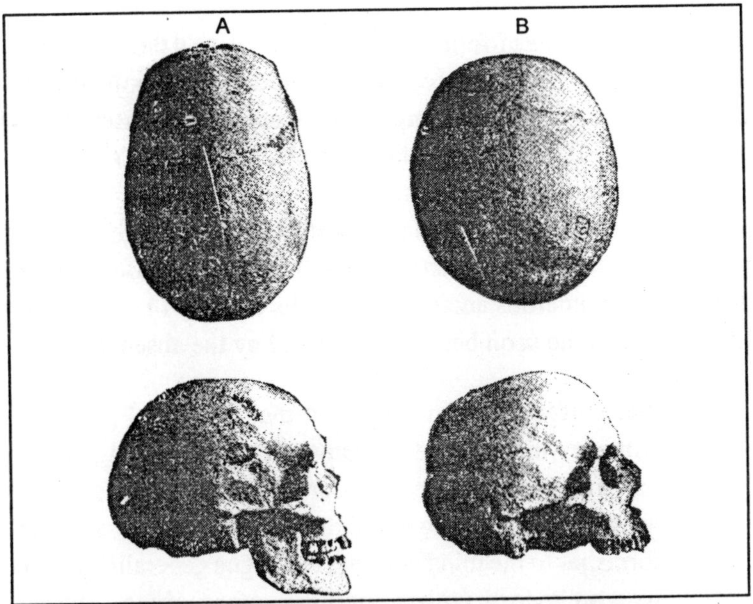

Fig. 2.2: Dolichocephalic and Brachycephalic Skulls belonging to Neolithic and Bronze Age races; photographed by the author from specimens in the Cambridge Anatomical Museum.

A. Long Barrow, Dinnington, Rotherham. Length, 204 mm.; breadth, 143 mm.; cranial index, 70.1.

B. Winterbourne Stoke. Length 177 mm.; breadth 156 mm.; cranial index, 88.1.

these three media—seeds, shot, and water—are still employed by craniologists.

In 1840 Retzius (1796-1860) introduced his theory regarding cranial shapes to the Academy of Science at Stockholm, and two years later gave a course of lectures on the same subject. He criticized the results attained by Blumenbach, showing that his group contains varying types of skull form; and he invented the cephalic index, or length-breadth index—*i.e.* the ratio of the breadth of a skull to its length, expressed as a percentage. The narrower skulls he termed dolichocephalic, the broader onces brachycephalic. By this method Retzius designed rather to arrange the forms of crania than to classify thereby the races of mankind, though he tried to group the European peoples more or less according to their head-form. While thus elaborating the suggestion of Blumenbach, he also recorded the degree of the projection of the jaws, demonstrated by Camper, and he added the measurements of the face, height, and jugular breadth. Thus was Craniology established on its present lines.

John Grattan (1800-1871), a Belfast apothecary, has never received the recognition that was his due. Having undertaken to describe the numerous ancient Irish skulls collected by his friend Edmund Getty, he soon became impressed by the absence of

> that uniformity of method and that numerical precision without which no scientific investigation requiring the co-operation of numerous observers can be successfully prosecuted. The mode of procedure hitherto adopted furnishes to the mind nothing, but vague generalities. until we can record with something approaching towards accuracy the proportional development of the great subdivisions of the brain, as indicated by its bony covering, and by our figures convey to the mind determinate ideas of the relation they bear towards each other, we shall not be in a position to do justice to our materials.... No single cranium can *per se* be taken to represent the true average characteristics of the variety from which it may be derived. It is only from a large deduction that the ethnologist can venture to pronounce with confidence upon the normal type of any race.[8]

Grattan devised a series of radial measurements from the *meatus auditorius,* and constructed an ingenious craniometer. As Professor J. Symington points out, "Grattan's work was almost contemporaneous with that of Anders Retzius, and nearly all of it was done before the German and French Schools had elaborated their schemes of skull measurements."[9] He adopted the most useful of the measurements then existing, and added new ones of his own devising.

The distinguished American physician and physiologist Dr. J. Aitken Meigs laid down the principle that "cranial measurements, to be of practical use, should be both absolute and relative. Absolute measurements are necessary to demonstrate those anatomical differences between the crania of different races which assume a great zoological significance in proportion to their constancy. By relative measurement of the head we obtain an approximate idea of the peculiar physiological character of the inclosed brain…the craniographer, in fact, becomes the cranioscopist."[10] In this paper Meigs gives craniometrical directions, some of which were designed to give measurements for portions of the brain.

Fig. 2.3: Paul Broca

In France the greatest names are those of Broca, Topinard, and de Quatrefages. Pierre Paul Broca (1824-1880) early in life distinguished himself, especially in surgery, not only in practical work but also in his writings. in 1847 he was appointed to serve on a Commission to report on some excavations in the cemetery of the Celestins, and this led him to study craniology, and thence to ethnology, in which his interest, once roused, never flagged. The story of the formation of the Société d'anthropologie de Paris (1859) and of l'École d'anthropologie (1876), of both of which Broca was the moving spirit, affords a curious commentary on the suspicion in which Anthropology was held. To the success of the school he devoted all his energies, and during many years of anxiety he met and overcame all obstacles, and finally placed it in a secure position. He invented several instruments for the more accurate study of craniology, such as the occipital crochet, goniometer, and stereograph, and also standardized methods; but, dissatisfied with the inconclusiveness of mere cranial comparisons, he turned towards the end of his life to the study of the brain. He was an indefatigable worker, and his sudden death in his fifty-sixth year is attributed to cerebral exhaustion.

"Broca was a man," said Dr. Beddoe, "who positively radiated science and the love of science; no one could associate with him without catching a portion of the sacred flame. Topinard has been the Elisha of this Elijah."[11]

Paul Topinard (1830-1911), pupil, colleague, and friend of Broca, made valuable investigations on the living population of France, besides devoting much time to anthropometrical studies; but his greatest service has been the preparation and publication of *L'Anthropologie* (1876),[12] a guide for students and a manual of reference for travellers and others. In 1885 he published his classic *Éléments d'anthropologie générale,* which aimed at creating a new atmosphere for the science, breaking free from the traditions of the monogenists and polygenists, and incorporating the new ideas spread by Darwin and Haeckel. *L'Homme dans la Nature* appeared in 1891.

Armand de Quatrefages de Bréau (1810-1892) was not only a distinguished zoologist, but also Professor of Anthropology at the Paris Museum of Natural History. In 1867 he published *Rapport sur le progrès de l'Anthropologie,* "which reduces to a complete and intelligible system the abstruse and difficult, and to many the incomprehensible, science of anthropology, embracing, during his investigations, a wide range of topics, and arranging disjointed facts in due order, so as at once to evince their bearing upon the subject."[13] He published many other works, among them *Les Pygmées* (1887), *L'espèce humaine* (1877), *Histoire générale des races humaines* (1889), and, together with E.T.J. Hamy (1842-1908), the famous *Crania ethnica* (1875-1879). De Quatrefages was a man of strong convictions, and though very conservative was ever ready to hear the other side. When the claim for man's antiquity was generally derided he championed the cause, but he was never won over by any of the theories of evolution.

In Germany Rudolf Ludwig Karl Virchow (1821-1902) had already gained fame in the medical world, especially with regard to histology, pathology, and the study of epidemics, before he began his valuable contributions to the science of Anthropology.[14]

His first anthropological writings were some papers on cretinism (1851 and 1852), and from this date onwards his services to the science were very great. Much of his energy was also given to somatic anthropology, and in 1866 he started his investigations into prehistoric archaeology, combining scientific method with spadework.

For a long period there was a rage for skull measurements and numberless skulls were collected from all over the world. Anatomists devised new measurements and ingenious instruments for taking them, and an elaborate terminology was evolved; scores of lines, arcs, chords, and indices were devised for the discrimination of the skulls of different races, and even now when a new fossil skull is found new methods are often employed. L.H. Dudley Buxton and G.M. Morant have recently suggested a standardization of the technique of cranial measurements ("The Essential Craniological Technique").[15]

Professor G. Sergi[16] at one time proposed to banish measurements from craniology, and to rely solely on observational methods. He later modified his extreme position, while, as a result of his crusade, he has induced most anthropologists to pay more attention to the configuration of the skull, and some of his descriptive terms have come into common use.

It is significant that many of the earlier craniologists recognized that the really important problem before them was to gain a knowledge of the size and relative proportions of the various regions of the brain, this being a direct result of the phrenological studies then so much in vogue. When phrenology became discredited, this aspect of craniometry was largely neglected, but later it exhibited signs of a healthy revival, and the inner surface of the cranium is now regarded as more instructive than the outer, since it gives an indication of the main features of the outer surface of the brain.

The superficial macroscopic structure of the human brain of various races has been studied by numerous anatomists, the main interest of which to the anthropologists consists in the possibility of forming some conception of the relative mental ability of these races based upon the external appearance of the convolutions and the functional significance of the arrangement and size of the different elements of the brain.

Elliot Smith says:

> We are gradually acquiring from the study of the brain of the modern human child, in comparison with that of the anthropoid apes and the endocranial casts of fossil men, a clearly defined picture of the process of the evolution of the brain. It now becomes a matter of special interest to interpret the processes which went on in the brain to confer upon man his supreme distinction—the human intellect.[17]

In this lecture and in his *Essays on the Evolution of Man*[18] and his *Human History,* 1930, he shows how in the evolution of mammals the brain became modified in response to the increasing sensibility of the sense-organs, and especially to the increasing dominance of vision, which in the Primates was associated with manual dexterity and ultimately with the erect position. Changes took place in the distribution of certain nerve fibres, and the neopallium took control of the movements of the whole body, and this led to further integration, which formed the mechanism for higher mental activities.

Though for a time craniology was hailed as the magical means by which all ethnological tangles could be unravelled, measurements of other parts of the body were not ignored by those who recognized that the skull alone was insufficient to determine racial affinities. Thus detailed studies of the limbs, brain, and viscera were made, and craniology, shorn of its extravagant claims, took its legitimate place as one in a series of investigations.

One of the earliest workers in body-measurements was Charles White (1728-1813), who measured no less than fifty Negroes. "He discovered that the forearm of the Negro relatively to the upper arm is longer than the forearm of the European, and that a corresponding relationship exists between the ape and the Negro."[19] White has been claimed as the founder of anthropometry. S.T. Soemmering (1755-1830), however, had made use of measurements in his comparison of the anatomy of the Negro with the European.[20]

Such features as the nose and ears, pigmentation of the skin and eyes, and the like, began to be studied about the middle of the nineteenth century.

In 1861 the venerated Dr. John Beddoe (1826-1911) published a study of hair and eye colour in Ireland, and continued his researches in this fruitful held from time to time in various parts of the British Isles, and to a less extent on the continent of Europe.[21]

But it was on the Continent that this method of investigation was most ardently prosecuted; and the story of its political origin may here be briefly recounted, since the results were of great service to the science of Anthropometry.

During the bombardment of Paris, in the Franco-Prussian War, the Natural History Museum suffered some damage through shells; and soon afterwards the Director, de Quatrefages, published a pamphlet on *La Race prussienne* (1871). This was to show that the Prussians were not Teutonic at all, but were descended from the Finns, who were classed with the Lapps as alien Mongolian intruders into Europe. They were thus mere barbarians, with a hatred of a culture they could not appreciate; and their object in shelling the museum was "to take from this Paris they execrate, from this Babylon that they curse, one of its elements of superiority and attraction, hence our collections were doomed to perish." A reply was made by Professor Virchow, of Berlin, and the battle raged furiously. The significance of this controversy to Anthropometry lies in the fact that, instigated by Virchow in 1876, the German Government authorized an official census of the colour of the hair and eyes of 60,00,000 school children of the Empire—a census which served at once as a stimulus to and a model for further investigators.

This census had some amusing and unexpected results, quoted by Dr. Tylor[22] as illustrating the growth of legends:—

> No doubt many legends of the ancient world, though not really history, are myths which have arisen by reasoning on actual events, as definite as that which, some four years ago, was terrifying the peasant mind in North Germany, and especially in Posen. The report had spread far and wide that all Catholic children with black hair and blue eyes were to be sent out of the country, some said to Russia, while others declared that it was the King of Prussia who had been playing cards with the Sultan of Turkey, and had staked and lost 40,000 fair-haired, blue-eyed children; and there were Moors travelling about in covered carts to

> collect them; and the school-masters were helping, for they were to have five dollars for every child they handed over. For a time popular excitement was quite serious; the parents kept the children away from school and hid them, and when they appeared in the streets of the market-town the little ones clung to them with terrified looks.... One schoolmaster, who evidently knew his people, assured the terrified parents that it was only the children with blue hair and green eyes that were wanted—an explanation which sent them home quite comforted.[23]

Observations of external characters, combined with precise measurements, have now been made on a large scale in most European countries and elsewhere, and these methods are adopted on the better equipped anthropological expeditions. In this way a great deal of valuable material for study is being accumulated. Such investigations are especially valuable when a large number of different peoples or races are studied by the same observer, as the personal equation remains fairly constant; the recent study of numerous peoples of southern Asia by Baron E. Eickstedt affords a good example.

All the methods of physical anthropology have been carefully described and fully illustrated by Dr. Rudolf Martin (1864-1924) in his great *Lehrbuch der Anthropologie,* 1914. Various small handbooks have also been published by others.

Though no one character can be used for the purpose of race discrimination, yet a series of measurements on sufficiently large groups of subjects, together with observations on the nature of hair, the colour of the skin, hair, and eyes, the form of various organs, such as the nose and ears, and comparisons of a similar nature, are indispensable for the study of the races of mankind. It is only in this way that the mixtures within a population can be sorted out and their origins traced. By such means critical evidence can be afforded for the reconstruction of racial migrations the occurrence of which is postulated by other lines of inquiry.

Obviously, it is essential that the characters employed in this way should be stable and not subject to rapid modification.

The nasal index, which is dependent on the width of the nasal aperture, has been accepted by anthropologists as one of the most useful clues to racial type. Arthur Thomson and L.H. Dudley Buxton[24] have investigated the correlation between the breadth of the aperture and climatic conditions, and assert that "the nasal index loses much of its significance as a purely ethnic character, and is to be interpreted largely as evidence of the habitat occupied" (p. 112). A. Davies[25] has reconsidered their evidence, and states (p. 335) that: "The nasal index evolved under the influence of climate; like hair and skin colour, it may nevertheless become a persistent ethnic feature and a reliable criterion."

Considerable interest was caused by investigations carried out under the direction of Professor F. Boas entitled "*Changes in Bodily Form of Descendants of Immigrants*."[26] The more important conclusions arrived at by Boas were that: "The east European Hebrew, who has a very round head, becomes more long-headed; the south Italian, who in Italy has an exceedingly long head, becomes more short-headed; so that both approach a uniform type in this country, so far as the roundness of head is concerned," and this in a period of about ten years. In the *American Anthropologist,* 1912, p. 532, he discusses various criticisms and says: "that 1 find myself unable to give an explanation of the phenomena, and that all I try to do is to prove that certain explanations are impossible" (p. 555). In reference to this Golden-weiser (1933, p. 390) says: "Recent investigations have shown that physical environment is strangely potent in producing changes in racial types," but G. Sergi,[27] H.J. Fleure,[28] J. Deniker[29] and others have not accepted these conclusions, though Boas produced "New evidence in regard to the instability of human types."[30]

Not only have physical measurements been recorded, but the device of an "index" has been adopted which gives the ratio between two measurements, as in the cephalic index (p. 20). The averages or the means of series of indices obtained from one people have been compared with those obtained from other peoples; but this method is misleading, as there is frequently a very considerable range in any given series, and a mean gives a colourless conception of racial type, the only value of which is a ready standard of comparison, which, however, is full of pitfalls.

A further step in the advancement of anthropometric research was made when the extent and frequency of such deviations were recorded. At first this was done in a tabular manner by means of sedations, then curves were employed; a single peak was held to indicate purity of race, double peaks that two racial elements were concerned, a broad peak or plateau was interpreted as being due to race fusion. Dr. C.S. Myers[31] discusses these and other methods. "There can be little doubt that most of the many-peaked curves owe their irregularity to the inadequate number of individual measurements." He states:

> If physical anthropology is to be a science, its results *must* be capable of expression in mathematical formulae. generally speaking the study of living forms is passing from the descriptive to the quantitative aspect, and it is by experiment and observation on biometrical lines that future progress is clearly promised. Thanks to the recent work of Professor Karl Pearson, the proper start has at last been made.

Karl Pearson and his colleagues (as can be seen in the journal *Biometrika* and in the *Proceedings of the Royal Society,* vols. 59-66) have now elaborated statistical methods, and have attacked the problems of correlations between various structures. They employ the methods of standard variation, correlative coefficients, retrogression coefficient, and other biometric devices. Thus an anthropologist should have a considerable amount of mathematical ability.

It should be remembered that Quetelet was the first to apply the Gaussian Law of Error to human measurements in its elementary binomial form; in this he was followed by Sir Francis Galton (1822-1911), who was the first in this country to realize the importance of applying mathematical methods to anthropology. An interesting account of the genesis of his work in this direction is given in his *Memories of My Life* (1908). Similar work was soon undertaken by German and American investigators.

Galton studied other problems, such as heredity, the progress in which is noted by R. Ruggles Gates.[32] C.C. Hurst[33] says:

> The new science of genetics has confirmed and extended Darwin's law of natural selection and Mendel's laws of heredity, both experimentally and mathematically... and has resulted in the elevation of biology to the rank of an exact science.... Man, if he chooses, can, here and now, take a hand in creative evolution by creating new species of living organisms and replacing natural selection by human selection.... Man's own destiny depends entirely on his response to the new knowledge and on his intelligent application of these discoveries in the near and distant future.

The problem of race improvement, or Eugenics, has been studied for some time past, and in this country was mainly connected with the name of Sir Francis Galton, who as long ago as 1865 published his views on the subject. Eugenics has been defined as "the study of agencies under social control that may improve or impair the racial qualities of future generations, either physically or mentally." A eugenics laboratory has been established in University College, London, in connection with Karl Pearson's biometric laboratory. *The Eugenics Review* deals with these problems.

Finger-prints as a means of identification were first discovered in Europe by Purkenje, the Breslau physiologist (1823), who utilized them for classification, but the practical utility of the method was not appreciated. Sir William J. Herschel[34] of the Indian Civil Service, when in Bengal in 1858, adopted the method of hand-prints of natives as seals on official documents, and in 1877 officially introduced the use of fingerprints after seventeen years' experience of the value of the evidence they afforded. H. Faulds[35] began to study finger-prints in 1877. Sir Francis Galton's attention was drawn to the ridges on finger tips in 1888 and he put the study on a scientific basis;[36] he frankly admitted his great indebtedness to Herschel. The practicality and precision of this method of identification were rapidly appreciated after the publication of Galton's books, and it has been adopted in most civilized countries as a substitute for the measurements selected by A. Bertillon (1853-1914) for the purpose of the identification of criminals.

As in so many other matters, Europe has to yield priority to Asia. Dr. B. Laufer[37] points out that, while the people of ancient India employed finger-impressions ritually, there is no evidence that they were used to establish the identity of a person; he also refers to the Chinese evidence, and says that in the T'ang dynasty (A.D. 618-906) finger-prints were utilized for purposes of identification.

Lamentably little is known with accuracy about the physical and psychical effects of a mixture of human types, and it is yet to be determined how far the admitted unsatisfactory character of many half-caste populations is due to physiological or social causes.

There is a great dearth of sufficiently numerous and reliable observations and statistics concerning the effect of the environment upon small or large groups of human beings, a problem which interested Prof. W. Ridgeway.[38]

It is desirable that the physical fitness of people should be tested in order to see how they stand in relation to other people, and to discover any physical imperfections. This is especially important in the case of children, a subject which is receiving close attention. By means of such investigations early inclinations to various defects are discovered and treated, and valuable statistics are obtained which can not only be utilized for comparative purposes, but may form a basis for legislative measures. It is also a matter of importance to determine whether certain imperfections are due to diseased, abnormal, or other undesirable factors in their parentage; or whether they are the result of unfavourable environment. But in order that comparisons can be made, it is necessary to make similar investigations on the normal, capable, and healthy population.

The last fifty years have witnessed a great development in the study of physical and mental reactions to various artificial conditions under which people are now forced to live, and for this purpose the methods of anthropology have been employed.

As early as 1834, L.R. Villermé[39] investigated various classes of the population of Great Britain, comparing dwellers in the country with those of manufacturing districts and large cities. F.C. Shrubsall[40] applied this line of inquiry to the incidence of ailments, and E.G. Bowen[41] and others have followed on similar lines.

During recent years it has been recognized that certain glands discharge internal secretions, or hormones, which alter stature, length of limb, size of jaw, shape of nose, growth of hair, texture of skin, and other characters which are in the main those wherein one race of mankind differs from another. Sir Arthur Keith[42] suggests that racial characters are determined largely by the activity of the hormones and that the inherited condition of the glands provides a mechanism for the fixation of racial types. It must not be supposed that the facts adduced by Keith imply that such groups as Mongols or Negroes are in any sense pathological, but merely that for some reason or another certain ductless glands function in some respects more actively, or less so, in these than in other groups. It remains to be shown what conditions of life or nutrition induced the supposed increased or decreased production of the hormones in question, or whether the conditions were "sports" which have been fixed by heredity. It has yet to be proved that these hormones

Fig. 2.4: Arthur Keith

are alone responsible for all racial differentiation, though they may well be contributory factors.

The agglutination of the red corpuscles of human blood when mixed with the serum of another human being has been intensively studied for some twenty years,[43] and it has been established that there are four kinds or groups (O, A, B, AB) of human blood which are inherited in the typical Mendelian way. All races have a considerable percentage of group O, which is very high in certain marginal races; unmixed American Indians are pure O, and the proportion is particularly high for the Australians, among whom the remainder are A. In Asia as a whole there are 20 to 35 per cent. of O. The predominance of A over B groups is most marked in Western Europe, and it decreases towards the east and south. In many marginal peoples group A is uncommon, and B still more so. A provisional conclusion is that group O, as it is universal, may be a primitive character, and that the blood-group A is older than B, since it is much more widespread in primitive peoples.[44] The predominance of one, or two, of these groups in large geographical areas is very suggestive of a racial trait, and it was at first hoped that blood-groups would almost automatically sort out the races of man, but the evidence at our disposal is as yet insufficient to permit of definite scientific conclusions.

Hutton[45] suggests that the origin and distribution of the B factor may be sought in the broad-headed Eurasiatic race. It is interesting to note that the relative proportion of the B group with respect to A in Berlin and Leipzig is higher than in the Rhineland, and in Westphalia it is higher on the east side of the Elbe than on the west side; in these cases the greater proportion of B is due to the large Slav or Eurasiatic element in the populations. H. Woollard and J.B. Cleland[46] "Believe that its [the blood-group method] service lies in its numerical value and its simple but definite hereditary nature, thus testing the validity of some anthropological hypotheses and suggesting other explanations and inquiries."

Notes

1. Cunningham, *J.R.A.I.*, 1908, p. 26.
2. *North American Med.-Chir. Rev.*, 1861, p. 840.
3. *Cephalogenesis*, 1815.
4. *Ideen zur Philosophie der Geschichte der Menschheit*, 1784.
5. J.E. Doornik, *Wijsgeering natuurkundig*, etc., 1815.
6. *Phil. Trans. Roy. Soc.*, 1836, p. 504.
7. *Notice sur l'Élpaisseur du Crane humaine* etc.
8. J. Grattan, *Ulster Journal of Arch.*, VI, 1858; cf. I, 1853.
9. *Proc. Belfast Nat. Hist., and Phil. Soc.*, 1903-1904, pp. 19-40; cf. *Journ. Anat. and Physiol.*, XXXVIII, 1904, pp. 259-274.
10. *North American Med.-Chir. Rev.*, 1861, p. 857.
11. *Jourm. Anth. Inst.*, XX, 1891, p. 349.
12. *Anthropology*, English translation, London, 1877; new ed., 1890.
13. *Anth. Rev.*, 1869, p. 231.
14. Cf. O. Israel, *Smithsonian Report*, 1902; trans, from *Deutsche Rundshau*, 1902.

15. *J.R.A.I.*, LXIII, 1933, p. 19.
16. "Le varietà umane," *Atti Soc. romana d'antvop,* I, 1893, p. 1; trans. Smithsonian Misc. coll. XXVIII, No. 969. "Sur une nouvelle methode," etc., *Congres int. d'anth. Moscow,* 1893, II, p. 297.
17. *Early Man,* 1931, p. 32.
18. 2nd ed., 1927.
19. D.J. Cunningham, *J.R.A.I.*, XXXVIII, 1908, p. 22.
20. *Ueber die körpliche Verschiedenheit des Negers von Europaer*, 1785.
21. Cf. Bibliography, *Man,* 1911, No. 93.
22. *Rep. Brit. Ass.*, 1879, p. 389.
23. *Journ. Anth. Inst.*, IX, 1879, p. 245.
24. "Man's Nasal Index in Relation to Certain Climatic Conditions," *J.R.A.I.*, LIII, 1923, p. 92.
25. "A Re-survey of the Morphology of the Nose in Relation to Climate," *J.R.A.I.*, LXII, 1932, p. 337.
26. *The Immigration Commissions, Washington,* 1910, 1911, and published as a book in 1912.
27. *Atti. Soc. rom. di Antropologia,* 1912.
28 *Man,* 1914, No. 101.
29. *Les Races et les Peuples de la Terre*, 1926, p. 138.
30. *Proc. Nat. Acad, of Science,* II, 1916, p. 713; VI, 1920, p. 489.
31. "The Future of Anthropometry," *Journ. Anth. Inst.*, XXXIII, 1903, p. 36.
32. *Heredity and Eugenics*, 1923; *Heredity in Man*, 1929.
33. *The Mechanism of Creative Evolution*, 1932, pp. xi, xii.
34. *Nature,* XXIII, 1880, p. 23; LI, 1894, p. 77.
35. *Ibid.*, XXII, 1880, p. 605.
36. *Finger Prints*, 1892; *Finger-print Directories*, 1895, and cf. E.R. Henry, *Classification and Uses of Finger Prints*, 3rd ed., 1905.
37. "History of the Finger-print System", *Smithsonian Rep.*, 1912 (1913), p. 631.
38. *Journ. Roy. Anth. Inst.*, XL, 1910, p. 10.
39. *Ann. d'hygiene publique*, XII, p. 217.
40. "Physical Characters and Morbid Proclivities," *St. Bartholomew's Reports,* XXXIX, 1903.
41. "The Incidence of Phthisis in Relation to Race-type and Social Environment in South and West Wales." *J.R. Anth. Inst.*, LVIII, 1928, p. 363; (Central Wales), LXIII, 1933, p. 49.
42. "The Differentiation of Mankind into Racial Types, *Rep. Brit. Ass.*, 1919, p. 275, reprinted in *Nature,* CIV, 1919, and in *Smithsonian Rep.* 1919 (1921), p. 443 "The Evolution of the Human Races." *J.R. Anth. Inst.*, LVIII, 1928, p. 305 (with references on p. 311).
43 L. Lattes, *Individuality of the Blood,* translation by L.W.H. Bertie, 1932 (with an exhaustive bibliography).

44. R. Ruggles Gates, *Man,* 1933, No. 208, and cf. *Am. Journ. Physic. Anthrop.* 1929, XII, p. 475.
45. J.H. Hutton, *Census of India,* 1931, I, Pt. i; 1933, p. 451.
46. "Anthropology and Blood-grouping, with Special Reference to the Australian Aborigines," *Man,* 1929, No. 145.

References

Camper, P. *Dissertation physique de M. Pierre Camper sur les Différences réeles que présentent les Traits de Visage chez les Hommes de différents pays et de différents Ages,* 1791.

Villermé, L.R. "Sur la population de la Grande-Bretagne", *Ann. d'hygiéne pub.,* XII, p. 217, 1834; see also XIII, p. 344 (1835); XX, p. 28 (1843).

Chapter III
The Older Anthropological Controversies

A stimulating effect on Anthropology has been produced by the controversies in which it has continually been involved. Anthropology was regarded in the past as a somewhat anarchical subject, giving rise to views which might prove dangerous to Church and State.

The discussions of the earlier centuries were focused round the question of the origin of man, and from this highly debatable problem arose the two antagonistic groups of the monogenists, or orthodox school, deriving all mankind from a single pair, and the polygenists, who believed in a multiple origin.

Among the ancient philosophers the question of the origin of man was answered in various ways. Some, like Pythagoras, Plato, and Aristotle, believed that mankind had always existed, because there never could have been a beginning of things, relying on the scholastic argument that no bird could be produced without an egg, and no egg without a bird. Epicurus and Lucretius believed in a "fortuitous cause," a preparation of fat and slimy earth, with a long incubation of water and conjunction of heavenly and planetary bodies. Others, that men and animals "crawled out of the earth by chance," "like mushrooms or blite".

With the spread of Christianity the Mosaic cosmogony became generally adopted, and monogenism developed into an article of faith. The Church fulminated against those atheists who admitted doubts on the subject of Adam and Eve, or believed in the existence of antipodal man, or that man had existed for more than the 6,000 years allotted to him by Scripture. If the censure of the Church did not lead to recantation, the heretic was burnt. A seventeenth century divine, Dr. Lightfoot, Vice-Chancellor of the University of Cambridge, was even more precise than Archbishop Ussher: he reached the conclusion that "man was created by the Trinity on October 23, 4004 B.C., at nine o'clock in the morning."[1]

The discovery of the New World dealt a severe blow to the authority of the Fathers on matters of science. Antipodal man, whom St. Augustine[2] had extinguished as "excessively absurd," has since been found to exist. Accepting the dictum of the Fathers, the Spaniards excused their barbarities to the American natives on the plea that they were not the descendants of Adam and Eve.

Henceforward the polygenists began to gain ground. Theophrastus Paracelsus (1520) first asserted the plurality of the races of mankind, and explained the Mosaic cosmogony as having been written "theologically, according to the faith, for the weaker brethren." Vanini (1616) mentions a belief, entertained by atheists, that man was descended from or allied to monkeys. In 1655 Isaac de la Peyrère, a Calvinist scholar of Bordeaux, published in Amsterdam his *Prae-Adamitae,* to prove that Adam and Eve were not the first human beings upon the earth; his work, being prohibited by authority, became immensely popular.

He regarded Adam and Eve as merely a special and later creation; the Gentiles, who peopled the rest of the earth, having been formed from the dust together with the beasts of the field, on the sixth day[3]. The inhabitants of the New World were necessarily of Gentile origin. The *Parlement* of Paris caused the book to be publicly burned. The Inquisition laid hands on the author, and he was forced to abjure both his Pre-Adamite heresy and his Calvinism. He died in a convent in 1676. This theory has lingered up to the present day. On entirely different grounds, there are some anatomists who regard the main groups of mankind as having arisen independently from simian ancestors.

The writings of the Encyclopedists, the freedom of thought claimed by Voltaire and Rousseau, together with the classification of species by Linnaeus, emboldened the polygenists. Lord Karnes[4] was one of the earliest exponents in England, and he soon found many followers. Two separate lines of antagonism may be distinguished in the controversy. In one—the Anglo-French—Prichard, Cuvier, and de Quatrefages represent the monogenists, and Virey and Bory de Saint-Vincent the polygenists; the other, in which America and the slavery question were implicated, polygenists and anti-abolitionists going hand-in-hand, was represented by J.C. Nott and G.R. Gliddon[5] in America, and Knox and Hunt in England.

Detrimental to the polygenist theory was what Broca termed *eugenesis—i.e.* that all the Hominidae are, and have always been, fertile with each other. At that time it was held that the crosses of species of animals and plants were infertile, so if human crosses were fertile, the parents all belonged to the same stock.

At first the monogenists claimed language as supporting their views, but it was soon found to be impossible to reconcile even the Aryan and Semitic languages to a common parent. Hovelacque and F. Müller and others held that distinct stock languages proved the existence of distinct stock races, but A.H. Keane[6] showed the absurdity of this line of argument.

Among the monogenists may be included most of the older anthropologists—Linnaeus, Buffon, Blumenbach, Camper, Prichard, and Lawrence. Since, they held that all mankind was descended from a single pair (the question whether this pair were white, black, or red occasioned a further discussion), they had to account for the subsequent divergence producing the present clearly-recognized varieties; in so doing they anticipated the theory of evolution, which was not clearly enunciated until the time of Lamarck.

Buffon ascribed the variations of man to the influence of climate and diet. Though Prichard and Lawrence both denied the possibility of the transmission of acquired characters, Prichard believed that the transmission of occasional variations might, to some extent, account for the diversities of races. Lawrence wrote more clearly: "Racial differences can be explained only by two principles—namely the occasional production of an offspring with different characters from those of the parents, as a native or congenital variety; and the propagation of such varieties by generation". He considered that domestication favoured the production of these congenital and transmissible variations, and, anticipating the Eugenic school, deplored the fact that, while so much care and attention was paid to the breeding of domestic animals, the breeding of man was left to the vagaries of his own individual fancy.

Sir William Lawrence's (1783-1867) lectures on *Comparative Anatomy, Physiology, Zoology, and the Natural History of Man,* delivered between 1816 and 1818 raised an immediate outcry, and he was charged with the "very unworthy design of propagating opinions detrimental to society, and of endeavouring to enforce them for the purpose of loosening those restraints in which the welfare of mankind depends." He announced publicly that the volumes had been suppressed as he was refused copyright. The *Lectures,* first published in 1819, reached a ninth edition in 1844. Lawrence was far in advance of his time, and much of his teaching may be said to have anticipated the doctrine of evolution. Unfortunately, the theological protest raised by his lectures—published when he was only thirty-five—resulted in his forsaking anthropology altogether.

Another man in advance of his times was Lord Monboddo. James Burnett Monboddo (1714-1790)[7] was regarded as one of the most eccentric characters of the eighteenth century, mainly on account of his peculiar views about the origin of society and of language and his theories as to the relationship of man with monkeys. He not only studied man as one of the animals, but he also studied savages with a view to elucidating the origin of civilization.

Many other pre-Darwinian evolutionists might be mentioned, but Professor Lovejoy's caution must be noted: "The premature adoption of a hypothesis is a sin against the scientific spirit; and the chance acceptance by some enthusiast of a truth in which, at the time, he has no sound reason for believing, by no means entitles him to any place of honour in the history of science."[8]

The first to enunciate a coherent theory of evolution—that of Transformism—was Lamarck (1744-1829). He believed that species were not fixed, but that the more complex were developed from simpler forms. He attributed this development to physical conditions of life, to crossing, and especially to use or disuse of organs. He also held that changes produced in the individual as the result of environment were transmitted to the offspring. Man formed no exception, he was the result of the slow transformation of certain apes. Lamarck's views were first published in 1801, and were enlarged in his *Philosophic zoologique,* 1809.

Lamarck's chief opponent was Cuvier (1769-1832), who upheld the theory of Catastrophe. According to this widely accepted belief, the universe was subject to violent terrestrial revolutions, involving the destruction of all living beings belonging to the past epoch, and the renewal each time of the flora and fauna by the incessant and miraculous intervention of a creative Will. The fact that mummified Egyptian animals dating back some three to four thousand years showed no appreciable difference from existing types was held to demolish the theory of evolution by proving the immutability of species.

Étienne Geoffrey Saint-Hilaire (1772-1844), the zoologist on the Egyptian expedition of 1801, interpreted the results differently and was one of the most brilliant supporters of Lamarck.

In 1844 appeared the anonymous book *Vestiges of the Natural History of Creation,* which had enormous influence on the pre-Darwinian history of Evolution. It was only on the publication of the twelfth edition in 1884 that it was known to have been written by Robert Chambers (1802-1871). In it was enunciated much of what was subsequently called the Darwinian theory. According to Wallace, it clearly formulated the conception of evolution through natural laws, and yet it was denounced by those who soon after were to become the champions of Darwinism. Huxley confessed in 1887 that "the book simply irritated me by the prodigious ignorance and thoroughly unscientific habit of mind manifested by the writer."

About 1850 Herbert Spencer wrote: "The special creation belief had dropped out of my mind many years before, and I could not remain in a suspended state: acceptance of the only possible alternative was imperative."[9]

This suspended state, the "tätige Skepsis" of Goethe, was just what Huxley was enjoying: in his own words, "Reversing the apostolic precept to be all things to all men, I usually defended the tenability of received doctrines when I had to do with the transmutationists; and stood up for the possibility of transmutation among the orthodox."

The publication of the *Origin of Species* in 1859 by Charles Darwin (1809-1882) had a stimulating effect on biologists. Darwin's work may be summed up in the words of his loyal and self-effacing co-worker Alfred Russel Wallace: "Before Darwin's work appeared the great majority of naturalists, and almost without exception the whole literary and scientific world, held firmly to the belief that species were realities and had not been derived from other species... [but by]... special creation.... The idea of special creation or any altogether exceptional mode of production is absolutely extinct."[10]

The ferment provoked by the publication of the *Origin of Species* profoundly affected the nascent science of anthropology. Clarkson had started his agitation for the abolition of the slave trade about 1782, and during the early years of the nineteenth century many unsuccessful attempts were made to bring the system to an end in America, where feeling ran so high as to dissolve the Union in 1861. At home the question was hotly debated, and popular feeling was excited by the speeches of Clarkson and Wilber-force, and most of all by the publication of *Uncle Tom's Cabin* (1852). Being largely a question of race, anthropology was soon implicated, monogenists and polygenists naturally ranked themselves on opposite sides, and the Ethnological Society became a strong partisan of the philanthropists and abolitionists.

In the midst of the excitement James Hunt (1833-1869), President of the newly formed Anthropological Society, read (1863) his paper on "The Negro's Place in Nature."[11] After examining the evidence on the subject, he made several deductions, amongst which were: that the Negro is a different species from the European; that the analogies are far more numerous between the Negro and the ape than between the European and the ape; that the Negro is inferior intellectually to the European; that the Negro race can only be humanized and civilized by Europeans; that European civilization is not suited to the Negro's requirements or character (p. 52). A tremendous outcry greeted the publication of this paper, and increased the tension on the already strained relations between the two societies. Fierce denunciations from the "broad-brimmed school of philanthropists" were matched by equally vehement applause from the opposing camp. When Dr. Hunt died in 1869 it was stated in a New York paper that: "Dr. Hunt, in his own clear knowledge and brave enthusiasm, was doing more for humanity, for the welfare of mankind, and for the glory of God, than all the philosophers, humanitarians, philanthropists, statesmen, and, we may say, bishops and clergy of England together."

A serious discussion of the anatomical and psychological relation of the Negro to the European is still to the fore, especially in the United States of North America. As late as 1900 a book was published in America with the title, *The Negro a Beast; or In the Image of God....* "The Negro a beast, but created with articulate speech and hands, that he may be of service to his master—the

White man," by Charles Carroll. The publishers are "convinced that when this book is read... it will be to the minds of the American people like unto the voice of God." This preposterous book could appeal only to the ignorant and bigoted, and is mentioned merely as an extreme instance of the difficulties against which science has sometimes to contend when dealing with burning social questions.

Professor F. Boas believes that the negro in his physical and mental make-up is not similar to the European. "There is, however, no proof whatever that these differences signify any appreciable degree of inferiority of the negro... for these racial differences are much less than the range of variation found in either race considered by itself."[12]

The Darwinian controversy reopened the question as to Man's place in nature. Linnaeus (1758) included man and apes among the Primates. Cuvier divided the Mammiferes into nine groups, man being included in the Bimanes, and the apes and monkeys in the Quadrumanes. The most noteworthy attempt to put man in his place was made when Huxley published his *Evidence as to Man's Place in Nature* (1863), based on lectures given in 1860, in which he proved that man was more nearly allied to the higher apes than the latter were to the lower monkeys. Concerning this book, he wrote to Mr. E. Clodd, thirty years later, "that a very shrewd friend of mine [Sir William Lawrence] implored me not to publish, as it would certainly ruin all my prospects." Doubtless one reason why Huxley wrote the book was to impress upon the public that the evolution of man as an animal is perfectly comparable with that of other mammals, since Darwin only hinted in his *Origin of Species* (1859) that "Light will be thrown on the origin of man and his history" (p. 488). His silence, he confesses in the Introduction to the *Descent of Man* (1871), was due to the desire "not to add to the prejudices against his views."

Carl Vogt (1864), who like so many other zoologists then and since was led to study anthropology, pointed out that "the ape-type does not culminate in one, but in three, anthropoid apes." On examining the species of mankind and their history, he arrived at similar results.

In the second volume of his *Generelle Morphologie* (1866) Haeckel applied the theory of evolution to the whole organic kingdom, including man, and drew up the first "genealogical trees". This attempt was improved and treated in a more popular form in his *Natural History of Creation* (1868), and again in his *Evolution of Man* (1879), an enlarged edition of which was published in 1905.

There is now general agreement that man should be included in one of the several families that constitute the sub-order Anthropoidea of the order Primates and also that the family Hominidae consists of several genera.

Notes

1. E. Clodd (1840-1930), *Pioneers of Evolution from Thales to Huxley,* quoting from A.D. White, *History of the Warfare of Science with Theology in Christendom*, 1876.
2. *De Civitate Dei*, c. A.D. 415.
3. T. Bendyshe, "The History of Anthropology," *Mem. Anth. Soc.*, I, 1865, pp. 348, 353-355.
4. *Sketches on the History of Man,* 1774.
5. *Indigenous Races of the Earth*, 1857.
6. *Ethnology,* 1896, chap. VII.
7. *Origin and Progress of Language*, 1773; cf. A.O. Lovejoy, *Popular Science Monthly*, LXV, 1904, pp. 336 ff.
8. *Pop. Sci. Monthly*, 1909, p. 499.
9. D. Duncan, *Life and Letters of Herbert Spencer,* 1908, II, p. 317.
10. *Rep. Brit. Assoc.*, 1876.
11. *Mem. Anth. Soc,* I, 1865, p. 1; cf. *Anth. Rev.*, I, 1863, p. 386.
12. "Race Problems in America," *Science,* 1909, p. 842.

References

Darwin C. *The Expression of the Emotions in Man and Animals,* 1872.
Wallace, A.R. *Darwinism,* London, 1889.
White, C. *An Account of the Regular Gradation in Man* etc. 1799.

Chapter IV
The Unfolding of the Antiquity of Man

Ignorance and prejudice combined to assert that man was created a few thousand years ago in a state of physical perfection. The possibility of the discovery of fossil man was, therefore, inconceivable to most people, and those earlier writers who entertained the idea were generally inclined to deny it. Cuvier, limiting the age of the earth to the orthodox 6,000 years, had stated that fossil bones of man did not exist. Moreover, up to the time of his death (1832) nothing had been found to disturb this generally received opinion.

More than a hundred years before (1726), Professor Scheuchzer, of Zürich, had discovered his famous "*Homo diluvii testis*"—"Man, witness of the Flood"—and had described it as a "rare relic of the accursed race of the primitive world," exclaiming piously: "Melancholy skeleton of an old sinner, convert the hearts of modern reprobates!" His fossil was proved later to be that of a gigantic salamander, and fossil man was allowed to sleep for more than a century.

When the question was again raised, in the middle of the nineteenth century, evidence of human remains which hitherto had been disregarded assumed a new importance, and earlier finds were re-examined.

The first ancient human cranium was found at Cannstadt in 1700, but remained undescribed in the Stuttgart Museum for 135 years. In 1848 a skull was found at Gibraltar which had to wait for fifty-nine years before it was properly described;[1] in 1926 Miss D. Garrod excavated a child's skull of the same race.[2] A great stimulus was given in 1856 by the discovery of a skull-cap in a cave in a small ravine called Neanderthal on the river Dussel in Rhenish Prussia. By the intervention of Dr. Fuhlrott other bones were rescued which are now in Bonn. When the remains were first exhibited by Schaaffhausen at Bonn, doubts were freely expressed as to their human character. Later Virchow, being prejudiced, pronounced his opinion that the cranium was diseased. Broca declared it to be normal. Huxley (1863) recognized it as human and said it was the most ape-like ever discovered, and he placed it below the Australian in type. Later discoveries served in the main to confirm Huxley's opinion.

Another important find was that of two human skeletons discovered in 1886 at Spy, in Belgium, by de Puydt and Lohest,[3] with an associated fauna which included the woolly rhinoceros, mammoth, cave bear, hyena, etc., five of the nine species being extinct.

A number of fragments of skeletons were found by M. Gorjanovic-Kramberger in 1899 at Krapina in Croatia; the skulls show that alone of Neanderthal men these folk were broad-headed.[4]

A very important burial was found in 1908 in a cave at La Chapelle-aux-Saints, which was described in a masterly memoir by M. Boule.[5] The same year O. Hauser, a Swiss dealer, discovered in the cave of Le Moustier a skull of Neanderthal type which he sold at an exorbitant price to the Museum fur Völkerkunde in Berlin; it was described by Klaatsch. Several other remains were found, carefully excavated, and described by Frenchmen: La Ferressie (1909-12) and Peche de L'Azé, both in the Dordogne, by Peyrony; La Quina in Charente by H. Martin (1911, 1921).

In 1914 and in 1916 fragmentary human remains were found at Ehringsdorf, near Weimar, and in 1925 the greater part of a cranium was recovered in a travertine layer. These proved that men hunted the abundant game which roamed in the valley of the Ilm during the temperate period before the last, or Würm, great glaciation.

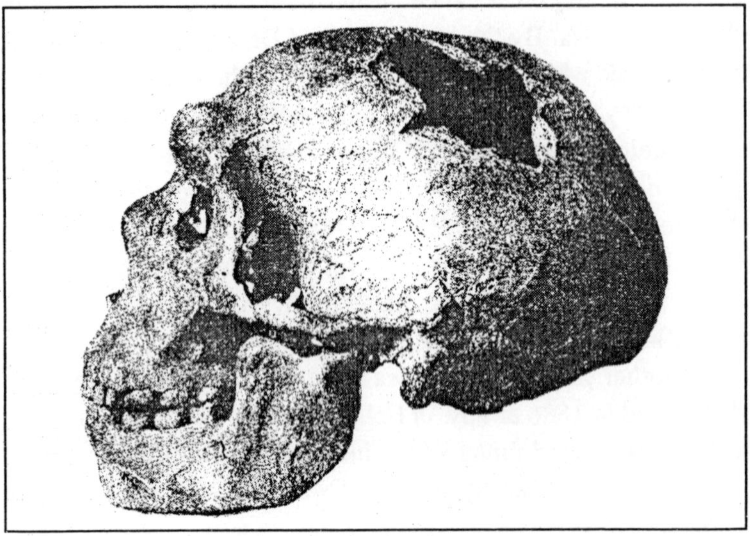

Fig. 4.1: Skull of the Fossil Man of La Chapelle-Aux-Saints
After the restoration of the nasal bones and jaws. From *L'Anthropologie*, XX, 1909, p. 267; with the permission of Professor M. Boule.

The La Chapelle man was of short stature (5 ft. 3 in.), but the skull is remarkably large. It is narrow, with a flattened cranial vault, has a receding forehead and very massive brow-ridges; the face is very projecting, the orbits large, and the nasal aperture broad.

All the foregoing remains are varieties, some very distinct, of the same stock of Man, to which the name *Homo neanderthalensis* was given by Prof. W. King of Galway, 1864. It is interesting to note that invariably these fossils were associated in Europe and Palestine with the Mousterian culture (p. 89), though it cannot yet be asserted that all tools of Mousterian type were made by this race. It is also worthy of mention that Neanderthal man has not been found in any deposit later than Mousterian times.

From early Pleistocene deposits, and therefore, much more ancient than the former, a human lower jaw was discovered at Mauer, near Heidelberg, in 1907. The teeth are typically human, but the massive, chinless jaw is neither distinctly human nor simian, but, as Boule remarks: "it would seem to have retained some aspects of a stage through which the common ancestor of anthropoid apes and man must have passed." Dr. O. Schœtensack named it *Homo heidelbergensis* (1908), whilst Bonarelli in 1909 erected for it a new genus, Palæoanthropus, in which Elliot Smith concurs.

All the foregoing are generally acknowledged as belonging to the genus Homo, but the startling discovery made by Dr. E. Dubois in Java in 1891, added a new genus to the Hominidae. Dr. Dubois received a thorough scientific training in Amsterdam, and, knowing that the Neanderthal men of the Middle Pleistocene were true men, he determined to endeavour to discover a "missing link". He realized that "many descendants of the Indian Pliocene (and earlier) mammalian fauna, especially such species as were adapted to a hot climate, must, at the time of the first glaciation of Northern India, have migrated to the more equatorial Indo-Malay sub-region," and expected to find there in the Pleistocene "lost types of the anthropoid Primates," some of which might be expected to be more man-like.[6] When searching the rich fossiliferous deposits below the dry-season level of the Bengawan River at Trinil, he discovered a tooth and then a skull-cap. The annual rise of the river in the rainy season inhibited further work, but in 1892 he found another tooth and a femur. Dubois published his account in Batavia, Java, in 1895, and named the new hominid *Pithecanthropus erectus.* Immediately a lively controversy ensued, and an extensive literature resulted to which practically every anatomist and anthropologist has contributed ever since. The problem resolved itself into three antagonistic points of view: whether the remains were simian, or human, or intermediate. The English, as Dr. Dubois somewhat slyly noted, clâimed the remains as human; while the Germans declared them to be simian; he himself, as a Dutchman, assigned them to be a mixture of both. From the capacity of the brain-case and the form of its interior, as well as for other reasons, Elliot Smith thinks "that Pithecanthropus is really a member, if a very lowly one, of the human family,"[7] and Dr. H. Weinert has critically discussed the whole problem,[8] with the result that he accepts it as belonging to the human family. There has also been a long discussion regarding its age; the present opinion points to its being lowermost Pleistocene.

Owing to the enthusiasm of Mr. C. Dawson, a lawyer, who was interested in collecting fossil remains, a very important discovery was made in a shallow gravel-pit at Piltdown in Sussex. He picked up in 1911 a fragment of a massive skull, next year he and Dr. Smith Woodward found the famous jaw and various other fragments, and in 1913 Pere Teilhard de Chardin found a canine tooth. The discoveries up to that date were announced in 1912 at the Geological Society of London, and, as was usual, led to a series of controversies. Sir Arthur Smith Woodward gave the hominid the name *Eoanthropus dawsoni,* and has fully described the remains in the *Quart. Journ. Geol. Soc.,* London, LXIX, 1913, p. 124. The skull has not the ferocious appearance of Neanderthal man, the brow-ridges are inconspicuous, and though the general appearance agrees with that of some types of modern man, the architecture is simian, as is also the jaw with its very large canine tooth; certain anatomists believed that it actually was the jaw of an unknown ape, but now everyone is agreed that the jaw belongs to the cranium. The interpretation of the internal cast of the cranium has led to great discussion; all that need be said is that the brain was at least as large as that of the average Australian, and was singularly defective in those parts which are associated with man's distinctive qualities (Elliot Smith). Sir Arthur Keith[9] goes so far as to say: "It is therefore possible that Piltdown man does represent the early Pleistocene ancestor of the modern type of man." The associated tools were made from flakes. The age of the gravel has been much disputed; it is generally believed to be of lower Pleistocene age.

In 1903 Professor Max Schlosser of Munich, by a brilliant line of reasoning, assigned a fossil tooth that had been sent to him from Peking to an unnamed new genus and species of anthropoid. In 1921 Dr. J.G. Andersson found a piece of quartz in a bone-bed near Peking, which he recognized must have been brought there by man. It was announced in 1926 that two human teeth had been discovered in a cave at Chou Kou Tien; next year another tooth was found, and on the strength of it Dr. Davidson Black created a new genus and species of the human family, *Sinanthropus pekinensis.*[10] Two jaws were found in 1928 which presented some simian characters and, though different from, they could be compared with, the Piltdown jaw. In 1929 Mr. W.C. Pei found a remarkably well-preserved brain-case, which was described by Davidson Black in *Palceontologica Sinica* in 1931. The cranium has a frontal region with prominent eyebrow ridges much resembling that of Pithecanthropus, but is more voluminous, while the posterior aspect, according to Elliot Smith, presents a definite likeness to Eoanthropus. There are features which do not occur in the other two types, and it may fairly be regarded as a representative of the original members of the human family which still retains traces of its simian ancestry.[11] It dates from the Lower Pleistocene. The associated stone implements have been described by W.C. Pei[12] and by Father Teilhard de Chardin and W.C. Pei;[13] they are essentially flake-tools most of which are of quartz. A complete account of these discoveries has recently been given by Davidson Black (1884-1934) and others.[14]

Professor Elliot Smith in his, *Search for Man's Ancestors,* 1931, has given most interesting accounts of the discoveries of the Java Man, Piltdown Man, and Peking Man, and the lessons to be learnt from these early remains.

Interesting fossil remains have been found in Africa in recent years. In 1924 Dr. R.B. Young discovered at Buxton, near Taungs in the Harts valley, Rhodesia, a skull which was described by Prof. R. Dart of Johannesburg and named by him *Australopithecus africanus.*[15] He regarded it as a representative of the pre-human stage of man's ancestry, but most anatomists consider it as a definite simian that had assumed certain incipient traits which are fully developed only in man. Dr. Broom considers it "quite likely to be Lower Pliocene" in age,[16] but others regard it as of Pleistocene age.

The enormous skull of unknown age found at Boskop, Transvaal, in 1913, described by S.H. Haughton[17] and by W.P. Pycraft,[18] was named *Homo capensis* by J. Hewitt in 1921. It is definitely neanthropic; the indices are analogous to those of Bushmen skulls, and it is possible that it represents the stock which gave rise to the somewhat degenerate Bushmen of recent times. This is rendered more probable by an intermediate type of skull which was discovered in 1017 by Mr. Peers in a cave at Skildergat, Cape Province, associated with the Still Bay culture, a contact-culture of flake-tools with a "Mousterian" industry. This Fish Hoek skull has been described by Keith (1931, p. 126).

Other fossil skulls have been found in South Africa, of which only two types can here be mentioned: the "Australoid" type has been found in four spots; its age is uncertain, but it probably belongs to the early Still Bay culture period. The significance of this interesting and probably ancient type is at present obscure. It is referred to by Boule and Vallois (1932, p. 74) and by Keith (1931, p. 140). The Springbok or Bushveld man (Broom, 1929) is considered by Keith as exhibiting affinities with Somali skulls (p. 152).

The most important skeleton in North-west Africa is that from Asselar in the Sahara, about 400 km. north-east of Timbuktu. It is probably of Upper Palaeolithic (Capsian) age, and has been described by M. Boule and H. Vallois,[19] who regard it as belonging to an old African type of man, ·ot related either to the Mediterraneans or Hamites, but as a representative of that stock which differentiated into the true Negro, the Bantu, the Hottentot, and the Bushman.

We have no unequivocal remains of the makers of the core-tools (Chellean, Acheulean etc.) of Europe. Dr. L.S.B. Leakey found in 1932 at Kanam in Kenya, near the north-east angle of Lake Victoria, a lower jaw which is sufficiently distinct from the *H. sapiens* type of jaw to be regarded as that of a new species, *Homo kanamensis;* it was associated with a roughly-chipped "pre-Chellean" pebble industry with an associated archaic fauna, and dates at latest from the beginning of the Lower Pleistocene. The skulls found at Kanjera are large, thick, very narrow, and low in the crown, and the brow ridges are not pronounced; they may be regarded as a generalized and rather primitive type of *Homo sapiens,* and they indicate an advance on Kanam man. They were associated with definite hand-axes (coups de poing), and were of Middle Pleistocene age. These discoveries of Dr. Leakey are startling and of the greatest importance, as they demonstrate the existence of the *Homo sapiens* type of man at an enormously more remote time than has hitherto been accepted.[20]

If the core-tool culture arose in Africa and spread thence to Western Europe, we would expect to find that the European implements were also made by a primitive type of *Homo sapiens,* as indeed has been suspected.

At Talgai on the Darling Downs, Queensland, a human skull of Pleistocene age was found in 1884, but it was exhibited only in 1914, and was described by Dr. S.A. Smith in the *Phil. Trans. Roy. Soc.,* Ser. B., Vol. 208, 1918, p. 351. It certainly belongs to an ancestor of the Australians, but presents more primitive features.[21] In 1925 a highly mineralized skull of the same race, but in better condition, was found at Cohuna, on the Murray River, Victoria.[22]

Although Dr. E. Dubois found two fossil human skulls at Wadjak in Java in 1890, it was not till 1920 that he described them.[23] They were of Pleistocene age, and bear such close resemblances to the Talgai skull that there can be no doubt that they are relics of the migration of the Proto-Australians from Asia to Australia.

Dr. A. Hrdlička has made careful investigation into the skeletal remains which have been attributed to early man in North and South America and into the stratigraphical evidence, and has come to the conclusion that many of the records were unsatisfactory and that, in any case, all the remains belonged to men of the modern type in America.[24] Keith[25] agrees with this, but adds that an exception may be made for the Punin skull of Pleistocene age from Ecuador, which has very marked "Australoid" characters. Numerous long, "low" skulls have been found in caves in South America; this Lagoa Santa type is certainly very different from that of the broad-headed existing peoples. In shell heaps in South America, and in California, long-headed skulls have been found which may be distinct from the former. Despite the opinion of Hrdlička, it would appear that the last word has not yet been said concerning the earliest peopling of America, a conclusion at which the cautious Dr. Boule has also arrived; and this is supported by recent research.

In the present state of our knowledge we can say that in early Pleistocene times there existed, but not synchronously, two hominids in the east of Asia and two in the west of Europe, all of which have been allocated to different genera. The Java man is admittedly the most primitive, the Peking man is more developed and seems to have a combination of characters of the former with those of a more advanced type. Piltdown man has a much more modern look despite his very simian jaw. The Heidelberg man is known only from his jaw. All of them retain more or less simian traits. This wide distribution at so early a date indicates that some sort of man must have existed in Pliocene times, and this is confirmed by Pliocene artifacts.

These human remains afford us suggestions as to the evolution of man, though some of them may have been merely alleys that led nowhere.

There are no data with regard to the evolutionary history of the ancient flake-tool makers in Europe or Asia.

Neanderthal man has always been found associated with Mousterian implements, but it is another matter whether all implements outside Europe termed "Mousterian" were made by that variable race of man. The original home of Neanderthal man has not yet been determined; perhaps it may prove to be in Asia. The Rhodesian man seems to belong to a branch of the stock from which Neanderthal man also sprang, but its age is uncertain.

It is generally admitted that in Western Europe Neanderthal man was suddenly replaced by modern or neanthropic man (*Homo sapiens),* though Hrdlička argues that the Neanderthal type was merely a phase through which *Homo sapiens* passed.[26] We know that makers of "Mousterian" and "Aurignacian" implements lived side by side in parts of Europe and Africa and in Palestine. There is evidence that neanthropic man with "Aurignacian" culture entered into Europe from Asia as well as from North-east Africa. Nothing is yet known about these supposed Asiatic immigrants, but some of the early Upper Palaeolithic men of Western Europe have certain African traits, and the "Aurignacian" (Capsian or Getulian) culture of North Africa was associated with a type of African man who ranged from North-west Africa to Kenya.

All that can here be said about neanthropic man is that whatever and wherever was his origin, he was a variable and energetic stock that soon spread over the whole world.

It is obvious from this brief survey that very little is really known about the past history of man, and it is equally evident that new discoveries will modify many of the current conclusions.

Notes

1. Sollas, *Phil. Trans. Roy. Soc,* 1907. B. cxcix, p. 281.
2. *J.R.A.I.,* LVIII, 1928, pp. 33-113.
3. Fraipont J. et Lohest, M., *Arch. de Biol.,* VII, 1887, p. 623.
4. *Der diluviale Mensch von Krapina in Kroatien,* 1906.
5. *Annates de paléontologie,* 1911-13, cf. *L'Anthropologie,* XIX, 1908, p. 519; XX, 1909, p. 257.

6. Elliot Smith, *The Search for Man's Ancestors*, 1931, p. 15.
7. *Proc. Brit. Acad.*, VII, 1917, p. 9.
8. *Zeit. f. Anat. u. Entwicklungsgesch.* Bd. 87, 1928.
9. *New Discoveries Relating to the Antiquity of Man*, 1931, p. 467.
10. *Pal. Sin.*, VII, 1927, p. 21.
11. Elliot Smith, *Antiquity,* V, 1931, p. 21; *Early Man,* 1931, p. 27.
12. *Bull. Geol. Soc. China*, XI, 1931, p. 109.
13. *Loc. cit.*, 1932, p. 315.
14. "Fossil Man in China," *Geol. Memoirs, Ser. A, No.* 11; *Geol. Survey of China*, 1933.
15. *Nature,* 1925, p. 195.
16. *Ibid.*, 1930, p. 814.
17. *Trans. R. Soc. S. Africa*, VI, 1917-18.
18. *J.R.A.I.*, LV, 1925, p. 179.
19. *Arch. l'Inst. Paléont. humaine, Mém.* 9, 1932.
20. *Man,* 1933, No. 210. These finds will be described in Dr. Leakey's forthcoming book *The Stone Age Races of Kenya,* Oxford, 1934.
21. Cf. Keith, *The Antiquity of Man,* 2nd ed., 1925, p. 448.
22. Keith, 1925, p. 304.
23. *Proc. K. Akad. van Wetensch te Amsterdam*, XXIII, pt. 7.
24. *Smithsonian Inst. Bull.*, No. 33, 1907; No. 52, 1912; No. 66, 1918; and Boule, *Fossil Men,* 1923, pp. 407-437.
25. *New Discoveries* etc., 1931, p. 311.
26. *J.R.A.I.*, LVII, 1927, p. 249.

References

Absolon, K., and Matiegka, J. "New finds of Fossil Human Skeletons in Moravia, etc.," *Anthropologie* (Prague), VII, 1929, p. 79.

Boule, M. *Les hommes fossiles,* Paris, 1921, 1923. *(Fossil Men,* translated from revised ed. of 1923), Edinburgh, 1923.

Drennen, M.R. "An Australoid Skull from the Cape Flats" [S. Africa], *Journ. Roy. Anth. Inst.*, LIX, 1929, p. 417.

Giesler, W., and Mollison, T. "Untersuchungen über den Oldowayfund." *Ver. Gesellsch. für physiche Anth.*, III, 1929, p. 50.

Hrdlička, A. "The most ancient Skeletal Remains of Man," *Smithsonian Rep. for 1913,* p. 491; reprinted 1916 (publication 2300).

Keith, Sir Arthur. *The Antiquity of Man,* 1915; 2nd ed., London, 1925.

_______, *New Discoveries Relating to the Antiquity of Man,* London, 1931.

Lyell, Sir Charles. *The Geological Evidence of the Antiquity of Man,* London, 1863.

McCurdy, G.C. *Human Origins,* New York, 1926.

Morant, G.M. "Studies of Palaeolithic Man," *Annals of Eugenics,* IV, 1930, pp. 109-214.

Obermaier, H. *El Hombre fósil,* Madrid, 1916. *Fossil Man in Spain,* New Haven, U.S.A., 1924.

Osborn, H.F. *Men of the Old Stone Age, 1915;* London, 3rd ed., 1918.

Pycraft, W.P., Smith, G. Elliot, and others. *Rhodesian Man and Associated Remains.* British Museum (Natural History), London, 1928.

Smith, G. Elliot. *The Evolution of Man,* London, 2nd ed., 1927.

______, *The Search for Man's Ancestors,* London, 1931.

______, Sollas, W.J. *Ancient Hunters,* 1911; London, 3rd ed., 1924.

Chapter V
Individual and Ethnic Psychology

At the present time the data for a comparison of the bodily functions of the members of one race with those of another are so scanty that the study of racial physiology can scarcely be said to exist. We are in a better position as regards comparative racial psychology, but a satisfactory technique has to be adopted before definite results can be established.

During the eighteenth century the term "anthropology" was often used to designate a consideration of the whole mental activities of man, as well as the relation between the soul and body. Later the centre of gravity shifted over to physical aspects of man, but anthropologists have always maintained their right to deal also with psychology.

Psychology in early times concerned itself with the essence of the soul considered as an independent entity, its relations to the body, its destructibility or indestructibility. The word psychology has always had a vague and varying signification.

In his retiring address to the Anthropological Society of London on January 1, 1867, Dr. James Hunt said:

> After a time, I think it will be found that the study of physical anthropology will be followed by researches in psychological anthropology. The believers in mesmerism now form a class as distinct from ordinary men of science as the phrenologists. They may have some valuable facts

> to communicate to science.... We do not wish to know what people believe, or what they think, but simply want empirically observed facts.[1]

Later in the year he read a paper "On Physio-Anthropology, its Aim and Method," which led to prolonged discussions; his aim was to pave the way for a rational psychology which would be serviceable for anthropologists.[2] It is interesting to note that forty years later the aspiration of James Hunt was realized in the work of his nephew W.H.R. Rivers. Even now the old phrenology still lingers, but mesmerism has been taken over by the psychologists.

During the last quarter of the last century a study of various obscure mental states received a fresh impetus in this country by the founding of the Society for Psychical Research. This society in the main has investigated: (1) Hypnotism, disorders of personality, automatic writing, crystal gazing, and the like, which are universally recognized as furnishing fields for scientific study alike among ourselves and alien peoples. The hypnotic and kindred practices of the lower races have until lately scarcely attracted the attention of anthropologists that their importance demands, although Andrew Lang said: "Anthropology must remain incomplete while it neglects this field, whether among wild or civilised men."[3] (2) Thought transference and its manifestations, which are not at present generally accepted as facts.

Order was only established in the physical world by ridding it of supernatural elements, and if we wish to understand the mental phenomena of witchcraft, modern spiritualism, and similar occult practices, it is necessary to eliminate supernatural considerations.

In 1869 L. Owen Pike perceived that "without psychology there is no anthropology,"[4] but it was not till many years later that this dictum was applied to fieldwork.

Experimental psychology was first seriously studied by G.T. Fechner.[5] A band of workers arose, and the new science spread to other countries. In our country Sir Francis Galton made a few psychological experiments on a large number of people from 1884 onwards, and now in nearly all of the larger universities in most countries experimental psychology is a recognized study, and almost every variety of mental condition is investigated. Professor W. Wundt has been a master builder on these foundations.

The experiments in laboratories were of necessity confined to subjects readily accessible, a few observations had been made on aliens, who, as a rule, had been brought from their native countries, and these were necessarily made under unfavourable conditions so far as the subject was concerned. A new departure was made in 1898 by the Cambridge Anthropological Expedition to Torres Straits. For the first time trained experimental psychologists (Drs. W.H.R. Rivers, W. McDougall, and C.S. Myers) investigated by means of adequate laboratory equipment a people in a low stage of culture under their ordinary conditions of life.[6] S.D. Porteus made a number of psycho-physical and intelligence tests on Australians in 1928-29, but most of the latter tests were scarcely suitable for these folk.[7]

The foregoing experiments were mainly designed as tests of sensory and mental efficiency of a particular group of natives which could be compared with results obtained from other races, but tests designed in psychological laboratories are often not justly applicable to a people whose interests are very different from those of highly civilized peoples, and who have become adapted to special conditions under which they exhibit a high degree of efficiency.

Professor R.W. Woodworth sums up the conclusions arrived at from his own observations and those of others as follows: "We are probably justified in inferring that the sensory and motor processes and the elementary brain activities, though differing in degree from one individual to another, are about the same from one race to another."[8]

The modern experimentalists in "behaviourism," building on the foundations laid by Fechner, Weber, Wundt, Cattell, Titchener,

Fig. 5.1: P.W.A. Bastian

and Stanley Hall, seem to be less interested in psychological processes than in the manner in which animals or humans respond to observable and measurable tests.

The recognition of the importance of psychology in ethnology owes much to the insistence of A. Bastian (1826-1905), who began in 1860 the first of a long series of writings in which he introduced the term *Elementargedanken,* the elementary ideas common to mankind; but these never found expression except in the form of *Völkergedanken,* folk ideas. He claimed that similar ideas and cultural features arose independently in many places and among diverse tribes, and also that such ideas and traits travelled from tribe to tribe and became incorporated in cultures other than those in which they had originated. The folk-ideas were originally circumscribed within areas, *Geographische Provinzen.* Bastian had a very obscure and involved style of writing, but he foreshadowed the cultural patterns and culture areas of later writers[9]. The psychic unity of man is admitted by psychologists, but it is quite another matter to affirm that men will think or act in the same manner under similar conditions. Prof. F.C. Bartlett[10] has written a valuable book on this subject.

A stimulating development in psychology has been accomplished by S. Freud and his school. Freud,[11] who had no training in normal psychology, emphasized the importance of the subconscious or unconscious in the ordering of human conduct, and defines the mechanism of the processes by which the subconscious takes effect and by which its workings are disguised, such as suppression, conversion, defence-reaction, compromise, formation, and the like. Psycho-analysis, in the hands of Freud and his disciples, discloses that the repressed urges of the unconscious are mostly or wholly sexual in character, but Rivers has emphasized that fear is quite as important.

In dealing with magic, Freud asserts that its basis lies in the mistaking of an imaginary connection for the real one, and that the whole animistic world, the realm of supernaturalism, is permeated by the "omnipotence of thought". He considers that some of the most widespread taboos are based on the unconscious. He insists that a substitution of ideas for things is a typical symptom of neurosis, and argues that the development of the psyche reproduces the transformations that have occurred in history. This led him to his theory of totemism; if the totem is the father in disguise, then not to kill the totem nor to marry a woman of the same totem can be explained by the two crimes of Oedipus, who killed his father and married his mother. He holds that in very early times mankind lived in so-called Cyclopean families,[12] in which the females were monopolized by the old male. One day the sons revolted, killed the father, and ate him; tortured by remorse, they agreed to abstain from sexual relations with the women of the group. This is pure conjecture, upon which G. Roheim bases an elaborate study, *Australian Totemism: a Psycho-analytic Study in Anthropology*, 1925, but his deductions do not appeal to many ethnologists. Attention may be drawn to W.H.R. Rivers's *Instinct and the Unconscious*, 1922, and to C.G. Seligman on "The Unconscious in Relation to Anthropology."[13]

The psychology of the crowd, as explained by G. le Bon,[14] is illustrated by the mass-behaviour of all peoples.

The greatest exponent of folk-psychology was W. Wundt[15] (1832-1920). Wundt holds that the psychological foundations of cultures cannot be found in individuals, but that the group always actively cooperated in the production of activities and ideas. The group was the carrier of habit and tradition, and constrained the individual to the pattern historically transmitted by it. He was fully aware of the great importance of diffusion as a dynamic factor in cultural growth, the development of which was not universally uniform, but was due to the multiplicity of motives and purposive changes. Thus, the psychological study of the individual can never suffice to explain language, art, myth, or religion; the social factors must be taken into account as well as the interchange of ideas between the individuals of the group. Although he laid stress on the group, he opposed the idea of a folk-soul sponsored by Lazarus and Steinthal. The conception of a "group mind" is still discussed.[16]

A group of French sociologists following E. Durkheim[17] consider (as Rivers points out, 1926, p. 36) that the work of practically the whole body of English anthropologists suffers from the radical defect that it supposes social institutions to have arisen in consequence of the realization of primitive ideas logically kin to our own; these, they hold, have not been operative at all stages of man's history. They consider it wrong to suppose that the psychology of the civilized individual can be used to explain social facts, and especially those of primitive human society. They claim that social facts (which they term "things") are of a special order, and require their own special mode of explanation. In early society there was, as is exhibited in primitive societies today, a solidarity in the actions of men as members of a social group which gave those actions a specific character, and makes it illegitimate to suppose that they were directed by motives of the same order which actuate the individual. They assert that the explanation of the facts of early society is to be sought in social conditions which have as their psychological expression what they call collective representations. The psychological character of these collective representations has been formulated by Lévy-Bruhl. Valuable essays by Durkheim, Hubert, Mauss, and others can be found in *L'Année sociologique.*

Lévy-Bruhl[18] holds that primitive thought is quite different from that of civilized man in that: (1) It is under the dominance of what he terms the law of participation, which is an expression for a large body of facts that indicate that originally man did not possess the same conception of individuality as we do, and many people still believe in a connection between the dissevered parts of what once was a whole, and that by acting on a separated part they can influence the individual itself. (2) It is not subject to the law of contradiction, which dominates our own thought and logic; thus primitive man is not disturbed by what to us are obvious contradictions, and can hold opinions which seem to us to be wholly incompatible with one another; that is to say, he has a prelogical or mystical mentality. It must, however, be remembered that primitive peoples classify the facts of the universe in categories different from our own, and have different principles for the classification of social institutions, such as relationship and kinship, from those adopted by us. Granting their premises, primitive men are usually as logical in these as in other matters of everyday life, as all first-hand observers testify. Lévy-Bruhl makes far too little of primitive rationality on the one hand and of modern irrationality on the other. The differences in logical conclusions are due to the character of knowledge accumulated by preceding generations.

In his address on "The Science of Man: Its Needs and its Prospects" Karl Pearson[19] stated that folk psychology was the urgent problem of the day; for this a new technique is necessary, which "shall not consist in the mere statement of opinion on the facts observed, but shall follow, if possible with greater insight, the methods which are coming into use in epidemiology and psychology." He quotes from Galton's address of thirty-five years before: "Until the phenomena of any branch of knowledge have been submitted to measurement and number it cannot assume the status and dignity of a science" (p. 150), as Friar Roger Bacon and Leonardo da Vinci had long ago proclaimed.

In the United States of America, thanks to the influence of Boas (p. 116), psychology has been well recognized by students as an essential factor in ethnology. The noted ethnographer, R. Thurnwald, has studied natives in Melanesia, and elsewhere, as a trained psychologist. The chief exponent of ethnological psychology in this country was Rivers, who stated that "the final aim of the study of society is the explanation of social behaviour in terms of psychology" (1926, p. 5).

It is mainly by a knowledge of individual and social motives and feelings, and of their reactions of existing primitive communities, that an interpretation can be arrived at concerning the events of historical ethnology.

The many books which have been written on the character, and on the "souls," of various peoples are based on general subjective considerations; scientific evidence would be difficult to obtain.

Notes

1. *Anth. Rev.*, V, 1867, p. lxvii.
2. *Loc. cit.*, p. ccix.

3. The Making of Religion, 1898; 1900, p. ix.
4. *Anth. Rev.*, No. 28, 1870, p. xi.
5. *Elemente der Psychophysik*, 1860.
6. *Reports of the Expedition*, Vol. II; and cf. C.S. Myers, *A Text book of Experimental Psychology, An Introduction to Experimental Psychology*, 1911.
7. *The Psychology of a Primitive People*, 1931.
8. *Science*, XXXI, 1910, p. 179.
9. *Goldenweiser*, 1933, pp. 72, 122.
10. *Psychology and Primitive Culture*, Cambridge, 1923.
11. *Die Traumdeutung*, 1900. *Vorlesungen zur Einfuhrung in die Psychoanalyse*, I, 1916; II, 1917; III, 1918.
12. The Cyclopean family was invented by Atkinson *(Social Origins*, by Andrew Lang, and *Primal Law*, by J.J. Atkinson, 1903).
13. *Brit. Journ. Psychology*, XVIII, 1928, p. 373.
14. *La Foule, tr. The Crowd.*
15. *Völkerpsychologie*, 10 vols.; *Elemente der Völkerpsychologie*, 1912 (English trans, by E.K. Schaub, *Elements of Folk Psychology*, 1916 etc.).
16. *Brit. Journ. Psychology*, XVIII, Pt. 4, 1928.
17. *La Méthode sociologique; The Elementary Forms of the Religious Life*, trs. by J.W. Swain, 1915.
18. *Les Fonctions mentales dans les sociétés inférieures*, 1910; *La Mentalité primitive*, 1922; *L'âme primitive*, 1927. These were translated by Lilian A. Clare: *How Natives Think*, 1926; *Primitive Mentality*, 1923; *The "Soul" of the Primitive*, 1928.
19. *Rep. Brit. Assoc.*, 1920, p. 140.

References

Boas, F. *The Mind of Primitive Man*, 1911.

Goldenweiser, A.A. *History, Psychology, and Culture*, 1933.

McDougall, W. *An Introduction to Social Psychology*, 1908 (his "instincts" have been questioned).

Rivers, W.H.R. *Medicine, Magic, and Religion, The Lancet*, XCV, 1917, pp. 919-23, 959-64; *Psychology and Ethnology*, 1926.

Chapter VI
The Classification and Distribution of Man

After the age of race discrimination comes the age of race description and classification; and, as we should expect, this second stage is not reached until the close of the Dark Ages and the dawn of the Renaissance, when thought had been emancipated from the bondage of scholastic authority and stimulated by the new impulse which affected all forms of intellectual activity.

The first attempt at the classification of mankind was that of a French traveller, F. Bernier (1625-88), whose scheme appeared in an anonymous article in the *Journal des Scavans,* 1684, entitled "A New Division of the Earth, according to the Different Species or Races of Men who Inhabit It," etc.[1]

He distinguished "four or five species or races": (1) The inhabitants of Europe, North Africa (including the Egyptians), and a great part of Asia (including the Indians). He notes that the Egyptians and Indians are black or copper-coloured, but considered the complexion to be due to climate. (2) The Africans, with thick lips, squab noses, and black skins, due not to climate but to nature, with scanty beard and woolly hair. (3) The Asiatics not included in the first group, white, with "broad shoulders, a flat face, a small squab nose, little pig's-eyes long and deep-set, and three hairs of beard." (4) The Lapps, "little stunted creatures, with thick legs, large shoulders, short neck, and a face elongated immensely; very ugly, and partaking much of the bear... they are wretched animals."

He hesitates whether to put the Americans or the inhabitants of South Africa, who are unlike the Negroes, into a fifth class. The latter are probably the Hottentots or Bushmen, in spite of his statement that "some of the Dutch say they speak *turkey.*"

The next classification was that of Linnaeus. His service to anthropology by fixing the place of *Homo sapiens* in the animal kingdom has already been noted (p. 12). In the first edition of the *Systema Naturæ* (1735),[2] Man is classed as a quadruped, and, together with apes and sloths, constitutes the order Anthropomorpha. Four varieties of Homo are recorded: *H. Europæus albesc., Americanus rubesc., Asiaticus fuscus, Africanus nigr.* In the second edition (1740) Homo is divided into the same four varieties, which are distinguished by the colour of their skin, located severally, one in each of the then known continents—*Europæus albus, Americanus rubescens, Asiaticus fuscus* and *Africanus niger.*

In the tenth edition (1758) more divisions are recognized; the genus Homo consists of two species: 1. Sapiens—1. H. diurnus; *Ferus* [including hairy men without speech, who run about on all-fours, of which six records are given]. *Americanus*, 2. *Europæus,* β. *Asiaticus*, γ. *Afer,* δ. *Monstrosus,* ε. a, Alpini, small, Patagonici, large, b, *Monorchides:* Hottentotti. *Junceæ:* Europæ. c, *Macrocephali;* Chinenses. *Plagiocephali:* Canadenses. 2. Troglodytes, H. nocturnus, Homo sylvestris Orang Outang. This classification was retained in the twelfth edition (1772). In these two latter editions the genera Simia, Lemur, and Vespertilio were classed with Homo in the order Primates.

In *Fauna Suecica,* published in 1746, Linnaeus made a more detailed classification of the population of Sweden, recognizing the three main types, distinguished by their stature, and hair and eye colour. These were the Goths, tall, hair white and straight, iris of the eyes ashen blue; Finns, with muscular body, hair long and yellow, and dark iris; and Lapps, with small, thin body, straight black hair, and iris blackish.

Blumenbach (1775) based his classification not only on skin colour, but also on skull form. To the four groups of Linnæus he added a fifth, dividing the one species into five varieties—the Caucasian, the Mongolian, the Ethiopian, the American, and the Malayan. The last group (which he discarded in 1795) included the then little known Australian, Papuan, and pure Malay types.

Blumenbach was the originator of the unfortunate title "Caucasian"[3] to represent the typical European and the inhabitants of Western Asia and Northern Africa. He chose the name partly because the Caucasus produces the most beautiful race of men, and also on account of the fine Georgian skull in his collection; as Waitz points out, "without any intention on his part to express thereby an opinion as to the cradle of these peoples." It was unfortunate, since, as Ripley shows,[4] nowhere else in the world probably is found such a heterogeneity of physical types—the only one conspicuously missing being the fair-haired, blue-eyed European—and such a diversity of language, sixty-eight dialects being here jumbled together, and only one of (possibly) Aryan origin. The name "Caucasian" has, therefore, not led to clarification of ideas in the complex problem of European ethnology. Keane,[5] however, supports its use, saying: "Those who object to 'Caucasic. are apt to forget the vast field that has to be embraced by this single collective term.... Caucasic, when properly understood... cannot be dispensed with until a more suitable general term be discovered."

The next classification was that of Cuvier, who derived mankind from the three sons of Noah, Japhet being regarded as the parent of the Caucasic, Shem of the Mongolian, and Ham of the African races. The divergence of type between the three brothers is not explained, except that the blackness of the descendants of Ham was attributed to the curse imposed by Noah on Canaan, the son of Ham.[6]

Other classifications followed, the divisions varying from two species, white and black, Virey (1801), to the fifteen or sixteen of the polygenists, Desmoulins and Bory de Saint Vincent (1827).

In America L. Agassiz, an uncompromising opponent of evolution, asserted, in 1845,[7] the unity of mankind as a species; but in 1850,[8] we find him distributing eleven or twelve, in 1853 (in Nott and Gliddon) eight, human species in as many geographical and faunal provinces.[9] But, this theory had been previously promulgated by A. Desmoulins[10] (1826) and by Swainson.[11] As Waitz rightly says: "They are completely in error who, adopting the views of Agassiz, assume as many original types of mankind as there are typically different peoples on the globe" (1864, p. 203).

It was not until the nineteenth century that a really scientific method of classification was adopted. In the majority of these schemes the character of the hair was chosen as the primary race-characteristic.

The hair had already been studied by Heusinger (1822), by Blower of Philadelphia, and by Kölliker, the histologist, before the publication of Pruner Bey's classic memoir, read before the Paris Anthropological Society in 1863 and published in the same year. Dr. Pruner Bey claimed that the quality of the hair constituted one of the best means of race-identification, and even that "a single hair presenting the average form characteristic of the race might serve to define it."

Long before this, in 1827, Bory de Saint Vincent had chosen the hair as the chief test in race-classification, and divided mankind into the *Leiotrichi,* or straight-haired, and the *Ulotrichi,* or woolly-haired; but his classification was robbed of permanent scientific value by his inclusion as distinct races of such vague abstractions as "Scythians," "Neptunians," and "Columbians."

Isidore Geoffrey Saint-Hilaire in 1860 distributed thirteen secondary races among four principal races,[12] primarily according to the character of the hair and sub-divided according to the flatness or projection of the nose, skin-colour, the shape of the skull, and the character of the face.

T.H. Huxley (1825-1895) in 1879 proposed four principal types or chief modifications of mankind: Australoid, Negroid,

Xanthochroic, Mongoloid. He was "disposed to think that the Melanochroi are the result of an intermixture between the Xanthochroi and the Australoids.... It is to the Xanthochroi and Melanochroi, taken together, that the absurd denomination of 'Caucasian' is usually applied" (p. 409).[13]

Ernst Haeckel (1834-1919) adopted from F. Müller (1879): A. Ulotrichi (woolly-haired): 1. Lophocomi (tuft-haired), 2. Eriocomi (fleecy-haired); B. Lissotrichi (straight-haired), 3. Euthycomi (stiff-haired), 4. Euplocomi (wavy-haired). The distinction between 1 and 2 is unsound, and the inclusion of Australians in 3 is erroneous.

In 1885 P. Topinard tentatively made three main groups: Whites, leptorhine; Yellows, mesorhine; Blacks, platyrhine; subdivided by head-form (pp. 502, 303).

Sir William Flower (1831-1899) in 1885 adopted the old threefold classification: I. Ethiopian, Negroid, or Melanian: A. African or typical Negroes; B. Hottentots and Bushmen; C. Oceanic Negroes or Melanesians; D. Negritos. II. Mongolian or Xanthous: A. Eskimo; B. Typical Mongolian (including the Mongolo-Altaic and the Southern Mongolian groups); C. Malay; D. Brown Polynesians or Malayo-Polynesians; E. American Indians (excluding the Eskimo). III. Caucasian or "White": A. Xanthochroi; B. Melanochroi. As Flower himself says, this scheme of classification, "in its broad outlines, scarcely differs from that proposed by Cuvier nearly sixty years ago.... Still, it can only be looked upon as an approximation." Although he places skin-colour first, he tacitly admits its insufficiency as a main diagnostic character, and his three groups practically coincide with a classification based on the nature of the hair.[14]

A. de Quatrefages[15] suggested three "trunks," Black, Yellow, White, each with four "branches" and two "mixed races" with several divisions, but he recognized that this was not a satisfactory classification.

Further research encouraged the growing conviction that a pure race is practically non-existent. J. Deniker (1852-1918) in *The*

Races of Man (English ed. 1900) says: "Taking into account all the new data of anthropological science, I endeavoured, as do the botanists, to form natural groups by combining the different characters (colour of the skin, nature of the hair, stature, form of the head, of the nose etc.)." This results in the formation of seventeen ethnic groups, containing twenty-nine races, and these are ingeniously arranged (p. 289) in a two-dimensional grouping to show their affinities, which is a modification of his suggestive earlier scheme.[16] The classification given in 1900 is repeated in 1926.[17]

C.H. Stratz recognizes three human races based on the proportions of the body: I. Protomorphic: (i) Australian, Papuan, Bushman; (ii) American, Indonesian; (iii) Ainu, Vedda, Dravidian, Eskimo, African Pygmy. II. Archimorphic: Xanthoderm or yellow-skinned, Leucoderm or white-skinned, Melanoderm or black-skinned. III. Metamorphic: (i) Xantho-leucoderm, Malay and Polynesian; (ii) Melanoleucoderm, Sudano-Ethiopian.[18] This classification has been more or less adopted by Fritsch and others.

F. Boas in 1908 grouped mankind into an Indian Ocean (or negroid) race, and a Pacific Ocean (or mongoloid) race. Thus, he regarded the yellow and white peoples as belonging to one stock and the black peoples (Negroids and Australians) as belonging to another stock. Similarly, J. Ranke adopted a light race with straight hair, and a black race with woolly hair.[19]

A.C. Haddon[20] gave "an arrangement of the main groups of mankind" based on the character of the hair, head-form, colour of the skin, and stature, and pointed out "that these demarcations are purely arbitrary and are employed merely to facilitate comparison and classification" (p. 13); a distribution scheme based on skin, hair, and nose is given (p. 157).

G. Montandon in his *l'Ologenèse humaine,* 1928, considers that the primitive human species occupied the whole habitable surface of the earth, except perhaps America. The daughter species reduced their habitat in proportion and according to their differentiation by dichotomy. The species thus did not spread from centres, but have successively restricted their respective areas, though secondary migration has often taken place. He gives (p. 204), a diagram of the formation of the eight great races (sub-species) by hologenetic dichotomy. The main thesis of this valuable book has not yet been generally adopted.

The "pigeon-hole" system of classification had been discredited in the fourth edition of Prichard's *Natural History of Man,* edited and enlarged by Edwin Norris (1855), where on p. 644 it is stated that: "The different races of men are not distinguished from each other by strongly marked, uniform, and permanent distinctions.... All the diversities which exist are variable and pass into each other by insensible gradations." Haddon[21] says: "There are, however, groups of mankind that exhibit so many intermediate characters that it is often very difficult to classify them. These may be due to racial mixture through long periods of time, but we must always bear in mind that they may be undifferentiated stocks, relics of early man, who have not acquired distinctive traits in areas of characterization. There are various areas where these hypothetical undifferentiated stocks may persist." H.J. Fleure recognizes in Britain a type which seems almost certainly not to be a mixture of the tall, fair, long-heads and the short, dark, long-heads. "It is rather a case of differentiation which has reached neither the one goal nor the other."[22]

Notes

1. See T. Bendyshe, *Mem. Anth. Soc.,* I, 1865, p. 360.
2. These accounts have been taken from the original editions; but the reader is referred to the verbatim copy given by Bendyshe in the *Mem. Anth. Soc.,* I, 1865, pp. 421 ff.
3. *The Anthropological Treatises of Blumenbach,* translated by T. Bendyshe, 1865, pp. 265, 269.
4. *Races of Europe*, 1900, p. 436.
5. *Man Past and Present*, 1899, p. 447.

6. *Genesis* ix. 25.
7. Smith, 1850, *Unity of the Human Races*, p. 349.
8. *Christian Examiner*, Boston, July 1850.
9. J.C. Nott and G.R. Gliddon, *Indigenous Races of the Earth*, 1857, p. 618.
10. *Histoire naturelle* etc., 1826.
11. Treatise on the Geography and Classification of Animals, 1835.
12. *Les Races*, etc., Deniker, 1926, p. 358; cf. Topinard, *Eléments d'Anthropologic générate*, 1885, p. 264.
13. *Journ. Ethnol. Soc. N.S.*, II, 1870, p. 404, with a coloured map.
14. *Journ. Anth. Inst.*, XIV, p. 380 ff.
15. *Histoire générate des Races humaines*, 1889.
16. *Bull. Soc. d'Anth.*, XII, 1889, p. 320.
17. *Les races et les peuples de la terre*, p. 360.
18. *Arch. f. Anth.* 1904, p. 189.
19. *Der Mensch*, 1894; 3rd ed., 1912, p. 194.
20. *The Races of Man*, 1924 revised ed., 1929.
21. *The Races of Man*, 1929, p. 139.
22 *Eugenics Rev.*, XIV, 1922, p. 97, and cf. *J.R.A.I.*, L, pp. 39, 40.

References

Beddoe, J. *The Races of Britain*, London, 1885.

_______, *The Anthropological History of Europe*, London, 1893.

Biasutti, R. *Studi sulla distribuzione dei caratteri e dei tipi antropologici*, Memorie geografiche, VI, 1912.

Buxton, L.H. Dudley. *The Peoples of Asia*, London, 1925.

Deniker, J. *The Races of Man* (English ed.), London, 1900.

_______, *Les races et les peuples de la terre*, Paris, 1926.

Dixon, R.B. *The Racial History of Man*, New York, 1923.

Eickstedt, E. Freiherr von. *Rassenkunde und Rassengeschichte der Menschheit*, Stuttgart, 1934.

Fleure, H.J. *The Peoples of Europe*, London, 1922.

_______,*The Races of England and Wales*, London, 1923.

Giaffrida-Ruggeri, V. (1872-1921). *L'Uomo attuale una specie collectiva*, Roma, 1913.

Homo sapiens, Wien and Leipzig, 1913 (German translation from Italian).

_______, *Su l'origine dell'uomo*, 1921.

Gunther, H.F.K. *The Racial Elements of European History* (translation of *Rassenkunde Europas*, München, 1926; largely propaganda), London, 1927.

Haddon, A.C. *The Wanderings of Peoples*, Cambridge, 1911.

_______, *The Races of Man*, 1909, 1924; revised ed., Cambridge, 1929.

Huntingdon, E. *Civilization and Climate*, New Haven, 1915.

Keane, A.H. *Ethnology*, Cambridge, 1896.

Man Past and Present, Cambridge, 1899; revised ed., 1920.

_______, *The World's Peoples,* London, 1908.

Luschan, F.V. *Völker, Rassen, Sprachen,* Berlin, 1922. Montandon, G. *L'ologenese humaine,* Paris, 1928 (with a voluminous bibliography).

Ripley, W.Z. *The Races of Europe* (with a voluminous bibliography), London, 1900.

Sergi, G. *Europa: l'origine dei popoli europei e loro relazioni cox popoli d'Africa, d'Asia e d'Oveania,* Torino, 1908.

_______, *L'uomo,* Torino, 1911.

Wissler, C. *The Relation of Nature to Man in Aboriginal America,* New York, 1926.

Chapter VII
The History of Archaeological Discovery

At the time when Dr. Johnson was gibing at Lord Monboddo for his belief in man's simian affinities he summed up contemporary opinion in the statement: "All that is really known of the ancient state of Britain is contained in a few pages. We can know no more than what the old writers have told us."

But, it was not long before it was recognized that there was other evidence besides that of the "old writers." As Sir W.R. Wilde has pointed out: "We possess what cannot be falsified by the scribe, and, though styled prehistoric, they are far more truthfully historical than the writing that no doubt was largely interfered with, and which, if old, now requires a gloss to interpret it." Archaeological remains "are now, in their way, far more truthful than anything that could have been committed to writing, even if there were letters in that day."[1]

Much of this evidence already existed, but even when rightly interpreted it was for a long time ignored and scoffed at. The first attitude of incredulity was to a great extent justified by the doubtful character of the earlier finds, some of which later investigation has had to reject or to hold in suspense as "not proven". The next stage was more serious, and for a long time the new science was hampered by the accusation of irreligion. But "Anthropology," as Huxley pointed out, "has nothing to do with the truth or falsehood of religion." "Je suis naturaliste," said l'Abbé Bourgeois, "je ne fais pas de théologie."

As far back as the sixteenth century, flint implements had been discovered in various parts and proved as great a puzzle as the fossils which perplexed and tried the faith of the earlier geologists.

The uncultured folk of Europe recognized that the chipped arrow-heads which occasionally occur on the surface of the ground were the implements of an alien people, as the names "elf darts" and "fairy darts" imply, while students are aware that these were the implements of earlier populations, who are classed in folk-memory under the generic term of "fairies".

Typical neolithic axe-heads had attracted the attention of writers in the Middle Ages, such as Gesner and Agricola, who, as Sir John Evans informs us, regarded them as thunderbolts, a belief which is still widely spread over the Old World. But Mercati, physician to Clement VIII at the end of the sixteenth century, maintained that they were the arms of a primitive people unacquainted with metal. Certain later writers, as de Boot (1636) and la Peyrère (1655), also regarded them as of human workmanship.

In 1797 John Frere found flint implements at a depth of about twelve feet in a brick earth pit at Hoxne, Suffolk, and referred them to "a very remote period indeed...and to a people who had not the use of metals." But the discovery did not attract any interest, and the implements remained unnoticed for more than half a century, until Evans, returning from Abbeville in 1859, recognized their importance, and further excavations have proved their antiquity.[2]

In the new science of archaeology Denmark took the lead. In 1806 a Commission was appointed to make a scientific investigation into the history, natural history, and geology of the country; among the first problems met with were the dolmens and shell-mounds abounding in stone implements, which found no period in Danish history capable of accommodating them. History and the sagas were searched in vain. Meanwhile more and more of these prehistoric implements were brought to light, and the various sites were carefully examined. The nucleus of the collection of Prof. R. Nyerup was formed in 1810, and expanded into the Royal Danish Museum of Antiquities at Copenhagen. C.J. Thomsen held the post of curator from 1816 to 1865. He arranged and classified the collections according to their epoch of culture and chronological order, and thus established scientifically, what had previously been vaguely recognized, the sequence of the Stone, Bronze, and Iron Ages. His work was continued and elaborated by Prof. J.J.A. Worsaae, 1865 to 1885.

Another class of evidence which was of great importance in determining the prehistory of man was that derived from caves. Prof. W. Boyd Dawkins (1839-1929) points out in *Cave Hunting,* 1874, p. 11, that caverns in the Hartz Mountains and in Hungary and Franconia were exploited in the sixteenth and seventeenth centuries for "ebur fossile," or unicorn's horn, which was accounted a specific for many diseases. As the true nature of the drug gradually revealed itself, the German caves became famous for the remains of fossil hyenas, elephants, and other strange animals, which had been used for medicine. The geologists who subsequently searched for bones did not suspect the occurrence of man in such early times, and doubtless much of the evidence of man's early history was unwittingly destroyed.

The Franconian caves were explored towards the end of the eighteenth century, and described by Esper (1774), Rosemuller (1804), and Goldfuss (1810). The most famous of these was the cave of Gailenreuth. Here, for the first time, investigations were carried out systematically, and since the co-existence of man and extinct mammals was indicated, theories as to their significance filled the air.

In 1816, Prof. William Buckland of Oxford (1784-1856), afterwards Dean of Westminster, visited the: caves. In his *Reliquce Diluviance* (1823) he argued in favour of a universal deluge, a view which was widely held by geologists. Dr. Buckland was henceforward the acknowledged authority on bone caves, and to his disbelief in the contemporaneous existence of man with the cave animals may be traced much of the incredulity with which all evidence of early man in Britain was received for more than a generation.

So far but few traces of man's presence in the caves had been detected, and, when found, had generally been explained away as later intrusions, though human occupations had been proved in Franconia, in caves explored by Tournal, E. Dumas, de Christol, and Marcel de Serres in France in 1828-30, and by the discoveries of Dr. Schmerling in the caves of Liège about 1832. From these forty caves Dr. Schmerling found not only bones of extinct animals, but also a few human bones and a large number of bones and flint implements, which he attributed to human workmanship. Unfortunately, these discoveries were discredited by both Dr. Buckland and Sir Charles Lyell, but have since been fully substantiated by Dr. E.F. Dupont.[3]

Kent's Cavern, Torquay, has been the most famous of English caves. In 1825 the Rev. J. MacEnery, accompanied by Mr. Northmore and Dr. Buckland, discovered the tooth of a rhinoceros and a flint blade, the first one to be found in a British cave, and subsequently he found many other flint implements. Dr. Buckland was still unconvinced, and believed that the ancient Britons had scooped out ovens in the stalagmite, and that through them the flint implements had reached their position in the cave earth. Godwin-Austen carried on the work in 1840, and arrived at the same conclusions. In 1846 the Torquay Natural History Society appointed a committee of investigation, consisting of Pengelly and two others, who also confirmed MacEnery's discovery of flint implements in conjunction with extinct animals. Nevertheless, their evidence was not accepted. In Pengelly's words: "The scientific world… told us that our statements were impossible, and we simply responded with the remark that we had not said they were possible, only that they were true."[14]

The turning-point was reached in 1858, when Pengelly carefully examined a new cave at Brixham, Torbay; here he found flint implements associated with the remains of hyena, bear, rhinoceros, and mammoth in undisturbed red loam beneath a layer of stalagmite. He read a paper at the British Association at Leeds the same year, and was supported by Charles Lyell, Owen, Prestwich, and others; the contemporary existence of man with a Pleistocene fauna was thus firmly established.

E. Lartet (1801-1871) was the chief founder in France of the new science; he with Mr. Henry Christy excavated the caves of Aurignac (1861) and Perigord (1864). From that date there has been a continuous series of excavations that have made the French caves classic ground, and all students of prehistory acknowledge their indebtedness to E. Rivière, E. Piette, E. Cartailhac, L. Capitan, G. de Mortillet, l'Abbé Brèuil, Obermayer, and many others. It is largely due to the work of these brilliant Frenchmen that archaeological stratigraphy has been placed on a firm basis.

Boucher de Perthes (1783-1868) was early interested in cave exploration; later on he found implements *in situ* in the gravels at Abbeville, and in 1834 submitted his "first diluvial axes" and his deductions to the Société d'émulation d'Abbeville, of which he was president. The next year he brought the same evidence to Paris. In 1846 he published the first volume of his researches, but "contradictions, jeers, scorn, were unsparingly heaped upon the author." But Boucher de Perthes was undisturbed, and continued his researches. In 1854 Dr. Rigollet of Amiens found axes in gravels at Saint-Acheul, and associated himself wholeheartedly with Boucher de Perthes, whom he had formerly strenuously opposed.

In 1858 Hugh Falconer, the palaeontologist, visited Abbeville, and satisfied himself with regard to the conclusions arrived at by Boucher de Perthes. Acting on Falconer's suggestion, a party of English geologists visited Abbeville in the following year, among whom were Joseph Prestwich, Charles Lyell, and John Evans, and Arthur J. Evans, then a boy accompanying his father, had the good fortune to find one of the chipped flints *in situ.* This visit established the horizon of the flints beyond question. Though the English archaeologists and geologists, on the evidence of the Devonshire caves, were already convinced of the antiquity of man, it was some years before all French opposition was routed, although A. Gaudry in 1859 had himself extracted worked flints associated with extinct mammals in the gravels at Saint-Acheul.

Subsequently gravel and loam pits throughout Europe were sedulously searched, and innumerable flint implements have been discovered and studied, and general agreement has been reached concerning the succession of various types of tools, but there is still keen discussion about the relative ages of many deposits. The earliest English systematizer of prehistoric archaeology was Sir John Evans, who published his memorable work, *The Ancient Stone Implements, Weapons and Ornaments of Great Britain* in 1872; 2nd ed., 1897.

Another series of investigations that shared the work of unfolding the history of man in Europe was that dealing with ancient dwellings.

In 1839 Sir W.R. Wilde explored some of the Irish crannogs, or semi-artificial islands, usually made of layers of stone, logs, and sticks resting on *cluans* or islets in the lakes. The first to be explored was that at Lagore, Co. Meath, famous in ancient times as Loch Gobhair, and mentioned in the *Annals of the Four Masters* as having been plundered in the ninth and tenth centuries. By 1857 forty-six crannogs had been recorded, and Sir William recognized their significance in elucidating the history of early human occupation in Ireland.

The winter of 1853-54 happened to be particularly dry, and, in consequence, tracts of the shores of the Swiss lakes were laid bare and dry. The inhabitants of Ober Meilen, near Zurich, took advantage of this to enclose part of the foreshore, and various remains came to light—stumps of piles, stone and horn implements, etc. Dr. F. Keller hastened to explore the newly revealed area.

Fishermen had long before reported the existence of a submerged forest, the stumps of which fouled their nets. Dr. Keller discovered that the "submerged forest" was formed of sharpened piles driven into the ground at regular intervals, and he recognized here evidence of prehistoric human occupation, corresponding with that recently proved for Denmark. Pile dwellings were subsequently discovered in other lakes, which yielded animal remains, stone implements, pottery, human bones, and one piece of bronze. At first the evidence was merely ignored, then it was listened to but disregarded, or various ingenious explanations were made to explain it away.

Subsequently similar structures or artificial islets were found in North Italian lakes, and, much later still, artificial islets were discovered near Glastonbury in England.

Thus were the foundations of Archaeology laid, and numerous workers in every European country assisted towards the amassing and explanation of data, but there is very much more yet to learn. From time to time the available information is summed up in various books, of which an imperfect list is given later.

Tertiary Stone Implements

While the existence of a primitive type of man in Tertiary times is probable, no actual remains have as yet been found, and his presumed existence has to be deduced from artifacts.

The existence of Tertiary Man was advocated by l'Abbé Bourgeois (1819-1878), and he exhibited at the Second Congress of Archaeology and Prehistoric Anthropology at Paris in 1867, flint " implements" from Miocene beds at Thenay, near Tours. The beds were undoubtedly Miocene or Upper Oligocene, but grave doubts were expressed as to the specimens being artifacts. At the International Congress of Anthropology at Brussels in 1872 the discussion was renewed, again inconclusively, though G. de Mortillet expressed the opinion that the objects were made by a semi-human precursor of man, which he named *Homosimius bourgeoisii.* L. Capitan rejected them after studying a collection of 2,500 of these flints.[5] The Eocene flints at Bellé-Assize, Clermont (Oise), have been shown by Breuil to be natural fractures.[6]

Other reputed finds of Tertiary Man were those by C. Ribeiro in 1860 in the Upper Miocene at Otta in the Tagus valley, and by J.B. Rames in 1877 in beds of the same horizon at Puy Courny, Cantal. The French specimens have been much questioned, though Sollas, after discussing the evidence of other Cantal flints, thinks that the "balance of probabilities distinctly points to the conclusion" that they "are the work of an intelligent being." [7]

It is not always an easy matter to determine whether the flaking of a flint is due to natural or artificial causes, since a practical knowledge is required of the various methods of intentional flaking, whether by percussion or by pressure-flaking, and also an appreciation of natural fractures by earth-movements, river and sea action, thermal action, or the undesigned effects of artificial pressure.

Pliocene Stone Implements[8]

Reid Moir in 1910 collected flints from the base of the Red Crag near Ipswich (Upper Pliocene), among which were peculiar forms, termed rostro-carinate; these were accepted by Ray Lankester as genuine artifacts, but this view was, and still is, disputed by many authorities. In 1920 Reid Moir obtained an undoubted artifact from the Red Crag, and by his discoveries at the Foxhall pit he definitely established the occurrence of recognizable tools in that stratum. Despite adverse criticism, Reid Moir persevered in his careful exploration, and has triumphantly established his main conclusions. He now can distinguish by their condition, colour, and forms, four distinct groups of flint implements at the base of the Red Crag which can be assigned to various periods prior to that in which the Suffolk bone-bed, composed largely of sweepings of an ancient land surface, was accumulated.

Pleistocene Stone Implements

The Pleistocene or Quaternary period is co-terminous with the Great Ice Age, the final disappearance of which ushers in the recent period. It is known that man lived in Europe during the fluctuations in climate that are collectively known as the Ice Age, but it is obvious that in the glacial phases certain parts of the land were uninhabitable. Recent research has done much to elucidate the varying conditions under which men had to live, and archaeologists have studied the tools which were made; thus in various ways light has been thrown upon the mode of life, and even upon some of the customs of these early folk.

Mr. B. Harrison of Ightham, Kent (1837-1921), first discovered "eoliths" in the glacial or pre-glacial gravels that cap the plateaux of Kent. This was in 1885, and since then large numbers have been found there and elsewhere. These have been much criticized, and many archaeologists still refuse to accept them.[9]

Concerning the other types of European implements there is no doubt, and they fall into sequences of main types of which the relative ages are generally admitted. E. Lartet was the first to draw up a chronological classification of quaternary implements; this was elaborated by Gabriel de Mortillet in 1869, 1872, and 1881, and adopted with modifications by J. Déchélette.[10] Since then numerous archaeologists have given more precise accounts of the various industries, but it has been found that the successive industries as demonstrated for Western France are not strictly applicable to the rest of Europe.

Modification of various implements is noticeable as time progressed, which in some cases seems to have been an evolution in form or technique, but in many cases can definitely be attributed to the influence of neighbouring or intrusive cultures, it is on these lines that research is progressing.

Recent research shows that migrations of peoples with their several cultures have taken place since the earliest times throughout the western hemisphere, but doubtless there have been spreads of culture with very little racial movement.

A flake-tool technique in the earliest known human times extended across the whole of Eurasia, since flake-tools were made by Sinanthropus and Eoanthropus, and they characterized the still earlier Red Crag industry.

As O. Menghin[11] has shown, in Lower Palaeolithic times a predominantly flake-tool, or "uniface," technique extended from North China in the east to Northeastern France and the southern half of England in the west; the Cromer-bed industry was mainly of this type. It is associated in Europe with a more or less arctic climate and fauna. The development of the culture in Western Europe was through Pre-chellean and Clactonian to Mousterian, with the Levalloisian as a side-branch. A "Mousterian" is also found in Palestine. In North Africa a "Mousterian" or Aterian industry was evolved from the Levalloisian. Flake-tool makers spread down East Africa to South Africa and, as elsewhere, when in contact with the core-technique they developed an industry very like the Mousterian.

Throughout all Africa a core-tool, or "biface," is the oldest known technique, and the same applies to India; in Africa it developed from a chipped-pebble industry. In Western and Southern Europe and in the southern half of England, hand-axes or coups-de-poing, the most characteristic type of implement of that technique, were always associated with interglacial conditions and a warm or temperate fauna. We may, therefore, conclude that this culture entered Europe from Northwest Africa after the flake-tool culture was established there, but the two cultures overlapped to a varying degree throughout a very large area, and at various places and times one or the other predominated. The sequence of these cultures in Europe is Chellean, Acheulean, and Micoquian.

After Mousterian times the implements are typically, but not universally, blade-tools, which are a form of flake-technique. There is no doubt that a complex culture passed into America across

Behring Strait. The oldest of these cultures in Europe is the Aurignacian, and there is an indication that one wave of "Aurignacian" culture spread from Asia and another from North Africa, where it is known as Capsian or Getulian. The lower Capsian of Africa is commonly regarded as the origin of the lower Aurignacian or Capsian of Spain. This culture extended down East Africa to South Africa, and it occurs in India.

Leakey finds that the makers of "Kenya Mousterian" tools were living in the same area and at the same time as the "Kenya Aurignacians." Miss D. Garrod records a co-existence of "Mousterian" and "Aurignacian" in Palestine, and H. Balfour has shown that the stone industry of the extinct Tasmanians exhibits a commingling of Mousterioid and Aurignacioid types of implements.

The Solutrean culture appears to have arisen in East Central Europe through a contact of flake-tool makers with blade-tool makers, and the culture spread to parts of Western Europe north of the mountain zone. The characteristic tool is the laurel-leaf point. It may here be noted that similar conditions in South Algeria, the Congo, East Africa, and South Africa seem to have led to the development of very similar points, as M.C. Burkitt has pointed out,[12] but such points do not prove that a true Solutrean culture or Solutrean man penetrated into Africa.

The Magdalenian was a local development from the Aurignacian in France, with but slight extensions beyond. Elsewhere the Aurignacian continued to evolve.

The foregoing observations refer to the implements or other artifacts made by early man; these, combined with our knowledge of the various existing conditions, afford indications of the modes of life of the several peoples. The definite burials that have been discovered throw, but little light on their beliefs, though we may assume they believed in a continuity of life, for which the dead were provided with tools etc. The objects of art found in the rock shelters and caves of France and Spain of the Capsian, Aurignacian, and Magdalenian periods show that these were made, engraved, or painted by gifted peoples who had gone a long way in cultural development, though their material resources were very limited. It is for these peoples and their congeners elsewhere that Elliot Smith has introduced the term Neanthropic (*Homo sapiens*) in contrast with the Neanderthal and other lower ancient races of man.

The Mesolithic or Epipalaeolithic period of Europe was one of unfavourable climatic and geographical conditions. It is characterized by very small tools, or microliths; technically it may be regarded as a development of the Aurignacian. In Africa (where it developed from the Capsian) and in Southern Asia the physical conditions were genial, and bearers of Mesolithic culture spread down to South Africa and into India. Ultimately, the culture reached Australia, where there are traces of Mousterioid and Aurignacioid techniques, and there has been a later Neolithic spread.

The main cultures, in Europe are the Azilian, Tardenoisian, Maglemosian, Kitchen Midden (Ertebollean), and the Campignian. The last of these is characterized by the occurrence of much larger tools than those of the earlier cultures.

The characteristic tools of the Neolithic[13] or last Stone Age culture were the ground and polished axes, but most of the tools continued the old chipped technique. The culture spread slowly from the east to the west of Europe, mainly along the valley of the Danube, but the older stone cultures persisted in places well into the Metal Age. With its spread came agriculture, domestic animals, and well-made pottery, and thus this higher culture laid the foundation of the civilization of Europe. The inference is that the first makers of polished tools were acquainted with metal tools, though the spread of the former was far more rapid than that of the latter.

We are beginning to learn something definite about this period in Britain;[14] and, though in the early years of the century not a single type of pottery was recognized, we now know that there were at least two cultural migrations each bringing a distinctive type of pottery. The earlier, arriving from the south, is termed Windmill Hill ware and that from the east Peterborough ware. The Neolithic of mainland Europe is a complicated period.

The Neolithic was mainly confined in the Old World to Eurasia, it barely reached South Africa. It extended to the New World, and eventually polished tools spread all over Oceania.

Recent investigations have shown, as has been mentioned incidentally, that, within limits, all the main stone cultures of Europe also occur in Africa, though no strict chronological equation between them can as yet be demonstrated. The relation of the various European cultures to the various phases of the Ice Age is being established, and it is now recognized that the physical causes which produced glacial phases in Europe induced approximately corresponding pluvial phases over at least Northern and East Central Africa. This line of research has been studied by Wayland in Uganda, and particularly by Leakey in East Africa, and in this way a relative correlation can be made. There are indications that the same may be done for India.

The later cultural history of Eurasia is very intricate, and archaeological discovery has proceeded at an ever-increasing rate and with ever-increasing efficiency, until it has become almost impossible to keep abreast with it or with the new conclusions which are being promulgated. Fortunately, there are students who summarize or synthesize this information, and it is on them that those who are interested in the subject must rely.

So many books have been published during the past fifty years dealing with special or general archaeological discoveries that it is impossible to enumerate them.

The *Corridors of Time,* by H. Peake and H.J. Fleure, is a concise but readable series of small books which give a well-illustrated survey of the archaeology, cultural history, and movements of the peoples of Europe, Western Asia, and Egypt.

Archaeology, like all sciences, cannot be self-sufficing. The early time-history of man is a geological problem. The conditions under which men lived in early times are geographical questions, as it is essential to know the soil, as well as the contours and geographical features of past periods; these are now being studied, and will help to explain settlements and migrations. Climatology is also looking backwards, and offers suggestions for the occurrence and periodicity of those great climatic changes which have so profoundly influenced human history. The botanists help by describing the various floras that accompany geographical and climatic changes, an interesting recent development being the identification of pollen grains and the study of their prevalence in various recent and Pleistocene soils, and the identification of the remains of cultivated plants, more especially of cereals. Zoology determines the characters of the animals domesticated by, or associated with, man, and so affords evidence for migrations; and the study of extinct animals, or palaeontology, is essential for time-history. Chemistry lends invaluable aid towards the preservation of finds. All these co-operations are exemplified in recent literature. Photography from the air is proving itself of the greatest service, as it reveals details that otherwise are indiscernible; for this we are indebted to the prescience and insistence of O.G.S. Cravford. Very numerous photographs of air discoveries are given in the journal *Antiquity.* This new instrument for discovery and investigation has already produced amazing results, which are but a prelude to those which we confidently await in the future.

The most noteworthy features of the last thirty or so years is the interest taken in various departments of archaeology from stone implements to ancient civilizations. Not only have unaided enthusiastic individuals toiled, and groups worked under the supervision of experts or of societies and financed by subscriptions, grants from administrative funds or by wealthy persons, but also public bodies, particularly the greater museums, have organized expeditions; what is especially pleasant is that frequently they combine in such operations, dividing the credit and the spoil between them.

To a large extent the day of exploitation has passed, and excavators spend an enormous amount of time and skill in the effort to wrest from a site all that it can possibly teach. Though the main object of a "dig" may be to solve a definite problem, before that can be done the remains of later cultures usually have to be disturbed, and these too are carefully studied, lest evidence should be destroyed.

The amount of work accomplished has been, and is continuing to be, prodigious, and the results have been commensurate. From the Red-Crag at one end of the time-scale to the classical civilizations and more recent times at the other, the history of mankind is being unveiled; for this is the ultimate aim of all such endeavours. It is not merely the history of technical improvements, nor even of the origin, growth, and decline of civilizations, or of the clash or fusion of cultures that is being elucidated, but the objects recovered are being studied with a view to extract as far as possible from them their aesthetic and religious significance. As we now know, it was the sense organs and the brain that were mainly responsible for progressive evolution among mammals, and emphatically for human evolution, so in prehistory, protohistory, and history proper, interesting and important as the advances in technical knowledge and artistic skill may be, it is the elucidation of the social and mental motives behind these that is the ultimate goal.

Notes

1. *Rep. Brit. Assoc.*, 1874, p. 116.
2. *Rep. Brit. Assoc*, 1896, p. 400.
3. *Les Temps prehistoriques en Belgique*, 1871.
4. *Kent's Cavern*, 1876; Lecture delivered at Glasgow, 1875.
5. *Rev. de l'École d'Anthr.*, XI, 1901.
6. *L'Anthropologie*, XXI, 1910.
7. *Ancient Hunters*, 3rd ed., 1924, p. 98.
8. The accepted line of demarcation between the Pliocene and the Pleistocene is here followed, but this may require some modification in the future.

9. Cf. J. Prestwich, *J.A.I.*, XXI, 1892, p. 246.
10. *Manuel d'Archéologie*, I, 1908.
11. *Weltgeschichte der Steinzeit*, 1931.
12. *South Africa's Past in Stone and Paint*, 1928, pp. 86, 87.
13. Sir John Lubbock invented the terms "Neolithic" and "Palaeolithic," the former to distinguish the newer stone implements and their period from the older stone implements and their period. *Prehistoric Times,* London, 1865, p. 60.
14. Cf. Jacquetta Hawkes, *Antiquity,* VIII, 1934, p. 24.

References

Breuil, H. "L'Afrique préhistorique," *Cahiers d'art,* 1930, pp. 449-500.
Burkitt, M.C. *Prehistory,* Cambridge, 1921.
_______, *Our Early Ancestors,* Cambridge, 1926.
_______, *The Old Stone Age,* Cambridge, 1933.
_______, *South Africa's Past in Stone and Paint,* Cambridge, 1928.
Childe, V. Gordon. *The Dawn of European Civilization,* London, 1925.
_______, *The Most Ancient East,* London, 1928.
Clark, J.G.D. *The Mesolithic Age in Britain,* Cambridge, 1932.
Dawkins, W. Boyd. *Early Man in Britain,* London, 1880.
Déchelette, J. *Manuel d'Archéologie,* Paris, 1908.
Evans, J. *The Ancient Stone Implements, Weapons, and Ornaments of Great Britain,* 1872.
_______, *The Ancient Bronze Implements, etc.,* 1881.
Garrod, Dorothy A.E. *The Upper Palaeolithic Age in Britain,* Oxford, 1926.
Goodwin, A.J.H., and van Riet Lowe, C. "The Stone Age Cultures of South Africa," *Ann. S. African Mus.,* XXVII, 1929.
Johnson, J.P. *The Pre-historic Period in South Africa,* 2nd ed., London, 1912.
Jones, Neville. *The Stone Age in Rhodesia,* 1926.
Kendrick, T.D., and Hawkes, C.F.C. *Archæology in England and Wales,* 1914-1931, London, 1932.
Leakey, L.S.B. (and others). *The Stone Age Cultures of Kenya Colony,* Cambridge, 1931.
_______, *Adam's Ancestors,* London, 1934.
Macalister, R.A.S. *A Text-book of European Archaeology,* Cambridge, 1921.
McCurdy, G.C. *Human Origins,* New York, 1926.
Menghin, O. *Weltgeschichte der Steinzeit,* Wien, 1931.
Moir, J. Reid. "Discoveries at Foxhall," *Prehistoric Society of East Anglia,* I, 1911, pp. 17, 24; II, 1915, p. 12; III, 1921, p. 389.
_______, *Pre-Palaelithic Man,* Ipswich and London, 1920.
_______, *The Antiquity of Man in East Anglia,* Cambridge, 1927.
Mortillet, G. de. *La prehistorique antiquité de l'homme,* 1883.

Obermaier, H. *Fossil Man in Spain,* 1924.
Peake, H., and Fleure, H.J. *The Corridors of Time,* Oxford (I, 1927; VIII, 1933).
Péringuey, L. "The Stone Ages of South Africa," *Ann. S. Afr. Mus.*, VIII, 1912.
Sollas, W.J. *Ancient Hunters,* London, 1924.

Chapter VIII
Linguistics

Linguistics as a department of anthropology may be regarded from many points of view. To the evolutionist, language forms one of the tests dividing the Hominida from the other anthropoids; the somatologist is interested in correlating the phonetic system with the structure of the organs connected with the mechanism of speech; and the ethnologist studies language for the evidence it affords of ethnic affinity or social contact, or as a means of determining the grade of culture to which a particular people has attained, or, again, as a reflection of their character or their psychology.

Albert Gallatin (1761-1840), a Swiss naturalized in America and a prominent statesman, was dissatisfied with the groupings by physical characters in the case of the races of America, so he made a preliminary classification on the basis of language. Major J.W. Powell (1834-1902) and Dr. D.G. Brinton (1837-1890) elaborated the linguistic classification of the American Indians, and others have followed in their steps.

Classification by language had already been utilized by Wilhelm von Humboldt (1767-1835), whose great work was published posthumously in 1836-1840. The rise of the new science of philology gave a fresh impetus to this method of classification.

Baron Bunsen read a paper before the British Association in 1847 in which he sought to show that the whole of mankind could be classified according to language. At that date it was taken for granted that the study of comparative philology would be in future the only safe foundation for the study of anthropology.

The connection between linguistics and anthropology assumed its greatest importance in the middle of the nineteenth century, when the discoveries and theories of philologists were adopted wholesale to explain the problems of European ethnology, and the Aryan controversy was launched. "No other scientific question, with the exception, perhaps, of the doctrine of evolution, was ever so bitterly discussed or so infernally confounded at the hands of Chauvinistic or otherwise biassed writers," says W.Z. Ripley.[1]

In 1786 Sir William Jones had pointed out the relationship between Sanskrit, Greek, Latin, German, and Celtic, and suggested a common parentage, which was confirmed by Bopp in 1835. Unfortunately, a primitive unity of speech was held to imply a primitive unity of race.

The spread of this fallacy is usually attributed to F. Max Müller (1823-1900), whose charm of style and high reputation as a Sanskrit scholar did much to popularize the new science of philology. He invented the term "Aryan," which in itself contains two questionable assumptions—one linguistic, that the Indo-Iranian group of languages is older than its relatives; and the other geographical, that its "cradle" was in ancient Ariana, in Central Asia. He allowed himself occasionally the freedom to speak of the Aryan or the Semitic race, meaning the people who spoke Aryan or Semitic languages, but he wrote:

> To me an ethnologist who speaks of Aryan race, Aryan blood, Aryan eyes and hair, is as great a sinner as a linguist who speaks of a dolichocephalic dictionary or a brachycephalic grammar. It is worse than a Babylonian confusion of tongues—it is downright theft.[2] The phonologist should collect his evidence, arrange his classes, divide and combine.... His evidence is the evidence of language, and nothing else.... There ought to

> be no compromise between ethnological and phonological science.[3]

The protest was in vain. The question of the identity of the Aryan race was soon a subject of keen debate. The Germans claimed that the Aryans were tall, fair, and long-headed, the ancestors of the modern Teutons; and the French, mainly on cultural evidence, claimed that the language, together with the civilization, came into Europe with the Alpine race, which forms such a large element in the modern French population. The present recrudescence of the German view is an interesting psychological phenomenon which is having tragic consequences.

There are two ways in which linguistics may be studied as an aid to ethnology—first, with regard to structural analysis, by which linguistic affinities may be proved; secondly, by what has been called "linguistic palaeontology," or the study of root words, by means of which the original culture of a people may be ascertained. Philologists pushed both these methods too far, and it was over the question of the "Aryan cradle" that they were forced to relinquish their too ambitious claims.

At the beginning of the nineteenth century it was generally believed that our first ancestors were created in 4004 B.C. and spoke Hebrew, and that the origin of the European languages dated from the migration of Japhet from the plains of Shinar, *c.* 2247. The Asiatic origin of race and language was for long unchallenged. But in 1839 Omalius d'Halloy, followed by the brilliant Latham in 1851, began to cast doubts on the Asiatic "cradle," noting that the Asiatic languages had no real claim to be considered older than those of Europe, and that in many ways the Lithuanian and Armenian were the most archaic in the family. More important still was the work of Benfey,[4] who may be regarded as the originator of linguistic palaeontology, and who used its evidence to shift the original dispersal from Asia to Europe. Various philologists followed, employing different methods to prove different theories;

and the Aryan cradle was located in many parts of Europe and Asia, ranging from the Pamir plateau to the Baltic plains. Max Müller confessed in 1888 that "the evidence is so pliant that it is possible to make out a more or less plausible case" for almost any part of the world.

Professor Sayce[5] says: "Identity or relationship of language can prove nothing more than social contact.... Language is an aid to the historian, but not to the ethnologist." But, as A.H. Keane[6] points out, there are cases in which language infallibly proves the existence of ethnical elements which but for it would have been unsuspected—as, for example, in the case of the Basques of Europe.

Pater W. Schmidt, in his little book *Die Mon-Kmer Völker,* 1906, proposed a new linguistic family—the Austric, composed of Austroasiatic and Austronesian groups; the latter includes Indonesian, Melanesian, and Polynesian. This generalization has proved very fruitful for ethnology.

Notes

1. *The Races of Europe*, 1900, p. 453.
2. *Biographies of Words and the Home of the Aryas*, 1888, p. 120.
3. *Rep. Brit. Assoc.*, 1891, p. 787.
4. T. Benfey, in preface to Fick's Vergleichendes Wörterbuch der Indogemanischen Sprachen, 1868.
5. *Science of Language*, II, 1880, p. 317.
6. *Ethnology*, 1896, p. 204.

Chapter IX
The Growth of Ethnology

"Ethnology" has often been used as a term synonymous with "Anthropology" to cover the whole field of the science of man. It was in this sense that it first came into prominence, being chosen by W.F.M. Edwards as the title for the Société ethnologique de Paris in 1839. The society was mainly concerned with physical anthropology, and was especially interested in the origins and relationships of the historical races of Europe. The Ethnological Society, established in 1843 in London, met with a rival, the Anthropological Society of London in 1863; the two societies were amalgamated in 1873 as the Anthropological Institute of Great Britain and Ireland. The term "ethnology" is here employed as mainly equivalent to cultural anthropology.

Ethnologists in the past have directed their attention mainly to the sociology of backward peoples in the attempt to discover the conditions from which more advanced societies may have arisen, but they fully recognize the importance of contemporary sociology and admit that there is but an arbitrary distinction between these two subjects.

The material for the study of ethnology has always been with us, but the study itself is of very recent development. The data have been collected by innumerable travellers, their elucidation has mainly been accomplished in the study.

In the earliest times Herodotus may be cited as the most distinguished name in the former group, and Lucretius in the latter.

The writings of Herodotus (*c.* 480-425 B.C.) are a veritable storehouse of information from the highest civilizations down to the veriest savagery, and his work has lost none of its freshness or value through lapse of time. As a matter of fact, modern investigations, carried out in the areas treated of by him, more frequently confirm and amplify rather than refute his statements.

Lucretius (99 or 98-55 B.C.), the poet, teacher, and reformer, boldly declared that there was no Golden Age from which man has degenerated, but that his progress has continually been slowly upward from a condition of pure savagery:

> Arms of old were hands, nails and teeth and stones and boughs broken off from the forests, and flame and fire, as soon as they had become known. Afterwards the force of iron and copper was discovered; and the use of copper was known before that of iron, as its nature is easier to work and it is found in greater quantity. With copper they would labour the soil of the earth, with copper stir up the billows of war.... Then by slow steps the sword of iron gained ground and the make of the copper sickle became a byword; and with iron they began to plough through the earth's soil, and the struggles of wavering war were rendered equal.[1]

Doubtless these particular generalizations were based upon tales told by travellers in distant lands, and upon traditional lore, which, with the exception of the recently acquired archaeological evidence, is practically all upon which we now have to rely. The philosophic poet apprehended the significance of various facts, and welded them into a consistent theory of the development of culture, and thereby was the first evolutionary anthropologist.

Nor should the versatile Strabo (*c.* 63 B.C.–A.D. 21) be overlooked, who was interested in many things, from climate to botany, and from sport to Druidism and Brahmanism. His *Geography* contains much information on the early history and traditions of numerous peoples, their character, dress, dwellings, and mode of life.

In the writings of the earlier travellers (to mention but three names)—Marco Polo, in Cathay (1254-1323), Ibn Batuta (1304-1377), in Asia; and Joao de Barros (1496-1570), who was considered the greatest authority on Portuguese, African, and Asiatic travels of his time—and in the records of travels contained in collections such as those of Hakluyt (1552-1616), Purchas (1577-1626), and Pinkerton (1758-1826), much ethnological information can be sifted from among the marvellous tales. Sometimes, the marvellous tales themselves can, by ethnology, be interpreted in fact, as when the "tailed men" of the Nicobars are found to owe their origin to the tail-like method of wearing the loin-cloth.[2] These were followed by the travellers and explorers of the eighteenth century, who brought back a vast amount of new information, both physical and cultural, from the lands they visited. Among these the names of Admiral Byron, James Bruce, L.A. Bougainville, Sir John Barrow, Captain Cook and the two Forsters who accompanied him, de Lesseps, and Pallas may be mentioned.

Other sources of information were the works of the Jesuit missionaries of the sixteenth to the eighteenth centuries, such as José d'Acosta (1539-1600), J.F. Lafitau[3] (1670-1740), and F.X. de Charlevoix (1682-1761), who worked among the Canadian Indians, and M. Dobrizhoffer (1717-1791).

Next come the missionaries of the nineteenth century, such as William Ellis (1794-1872), who laboured in South Africa and Madagascar, but is best known for his work in Polynesia; John Williams (1796-1839); George Turner (1818-1891); W. Wyatt Gill (1828-1896), and others who also worked in the Pacific. In Africa we may mention Bishop Callaway (1817-1890) and David Livingstone (1813-1873). At the same time the Roman Catholjc missionary E.R. Hue (1813-1860) was working in China and Tartary, while the Abbe Dubois (1770-1848) was laboriously investigating the manners, customs, and ceremonies of the Hindus.

In response to the modern requirements of ethnology, the contributions of missionaries for the past fifty years have been increasingly valuable, as can be seen by the use that students make of them. To mention but a very few—Africa: H.A. Junod, John Roscoe (1861-1932), Edwin W. Smith. Australia: C. Streh-low. Especially may be noted those missionaries trained by Pater W. Schmidt, whose researches are published in *Anthropos.*

A deep debt of gratitude is owed to the explorers, travellers, and administrative officers in all parts of the world who collectively have provided a vast amount of information about the peoples among whom they have travelled or over whom they have ruled. Survey voyages and general scientific expeditions often collected valuable information, but the most satisfactory have been the various anthropological expeditions consisting of trained workers, who, besides amassing fresh evidence, checked, corrected, or amplified the work of earlier observers.

Such varied data, often of unequal value, have formed the foundation on which the science of ethnology has been and is being laboriously built. This material has been dealt with in various ways.

A German Professor of philosophy, Christoph Meiners (1747-1816), by noting the history of various ethnological data, ranging from food to government, pointed the way to comparative ethnology: *Grundriss der Geschichte der Menschheit* (Lemgo, 1785); *Unter-suchungen über die verschiedenen Menschennaturen (die verschiedenen Menschenarten)* (Tübingen, 1811). He emphasized the importance of racial purity.

The marshalling of a vast array of new observations and deductions required a broad mind, wide knowledge, and shrewd reasoning powers. These, together with a sound training in anatomy and unusual acquaintance with philology, and some eminence in psychology, produced the monumental work of Prichard.

James Cowles Prichard (1786-1848) as a boy lived in Bristol, and there began his practical study of anthropology by spending his time at the docks, watching the foreign sailors and chatting

Fig. 9.1: J.C. Prichard

with them in their own tongues. Later on he chose medicine for his profession, mainly because it afforded him opportunities for indulging in his anthropological tastes. His first contribution to science was his thesis for the degree of Doctor of Medicine at Edinburgh, entitled *De generis humani varietate,* which was published in 1813 in an expanded form as *Researches into the Physical History of Man.* It was still further expanded in 1826, and a five-volume edition was issued between 1836 and 1847. In 1843 appeared another monumental work, *The Natural History of Man; comprising inquiries into the modifying influence of physical and moral agencies on the different tribes of the human family.* Edwin Norris's edition appeared in 1855. In these books he gives detailed descriptions of all the races known to him, with various ethnological facts, but he did not give a racial classification. These works formed the corner-stones of anthropology in England.

At the same time Antoine Desmoulins was writing his *Histoire naturelle des races humaines,* 1826. He attempted to discover the origins and relations of the peoples of North-east Europe, North and East Asia, and South Africa, by the evidence of archaeology, physiology, anatomy, and linguistics.

Other works of systematization of the mass of anthropological data and reducing them into an orderly scheme continued to be produced. R.G. Latham (1812-1888), "a prodigy of learning" published his *Natural History of the Varieties of Man* in 1850 [the same year as R. Knox's (1791-1862) *Races of Man*], and his *Descriptive Ethnology* in 1859. In the latter year appeared the *Anthropologie der Naturvölker* of T. Waitz, the six volumes of which were completed in 1872 (Gerland's edition was published in 1877); a work which largely assisted in laying a secure foundation for the new science. The excellent *Natural History of Man* by J.G. Wood (1868, 1870) is an illustrated " account of the manners and customs of the uncivilized races of men," and may still be consulted with profit. In 1873 Friedrich Muller published his *Allgemeine Ethnographie.* The following year saw the publication of Peschel's *Völkerkunde.* F. Ratzel's (1844-1904) great and richly illustrated work *Völkerkunde* appeared in 1885-88, the second edition (1894-95) was translated by A.J. Butler under the misleading title of *The History of Mankind* (1896). Reference may also be given to A.H. Keane in his *Man Past and Present* (1899, revised ed., 1920). J. Deniker's *Les races et les peuples de la terre,* together with the English translation, appeared in 1900, and an enlarged edition in 1926. Of great value is the *Illustrierte Völkerkunde,* by G. Buschan, of which an enlarged edition was issued in 1923.

The question as to the influence of environment on man was discussed by the above-mentioned systematizes, and its effect upon his material culture, social groupings, religion, and the like, was noted from the earliest times, and for a hundred years has received much attention.

Hippocrates (*c.* 460-377 B.C.), in his work *De aëre, aquis, et locis,* discussed the influence of environment on man, physical, moral, and pathological. He divided mankind into groups, impressed with homogeneous characters by homogeneous surroundings, demonstrating that mountains, plains, damp, aridity, and so on, produced definite and varied types. J.M. Robertson notes that "theories of the influence of climate on character were common in antiquity," and refers to Vitruvius (VI, 1), Vegetius *(De re militari,* 1, 2) and Servius (on Vergil, *Aeneid,* VI, 724).[4]

Bodin (1530-96) wrote in 1576 a book[5] which contains, as J.L. Myres has pointed out,[6] "the whole pith and kernel of modern anthropogeography.... His climatic contrasts are based on the Ptolemaic geography... and argues as if the world broke off short at Sahara.... On his classification of environments from arctic North to tropic South" he superposes "a cross-division by grades of culture from civil East to barbaric West." He held, however, that reason is common to all men, and is not subject to the environment, and thus he escaped the extreme views of nature's compelling influence over man on the one hand and of man's total independence of nature on the other. Man, he emphasized, is morally free from environmental control. The circumambient medium determines only the development of man's capabilities. Man can counteract, and may, even though with difficulty, overcome the injurious action of climate and nature.[7]

Montesquieu,[8] apparently without acknowledgment, adopted the views of Bodin, but it was due to him that they received the general acceptance of educated Europe.[9] Flint[10] points out that A.R.J. Turgot (1727-81) in his sketch of a "Political Geography," had attained to a broader view of the relationship of human development to the features of the earth and to physical agencies in general than even Montesquieu, and saw that many of Montesquieu's inductions were premature and inadequate.

Buffon followed Hippocrates. Man, said he, consists of a single species. Individual variations are due to three causes—climate, food, and habits. These influences, acting over large areas on large groups of people, produce general and constant varieties, to which he gave the name "races".

The recognition of environmental influences has long been a characteristic of the French. A great stimulus in this direction was given by the school of Le Play (1806-1882) in France, the concrete application of whose methods was worked out by E. Demolins and others, and published in the journal *La Science Sociale* and in separate works. It is the essential procedure of this school of descriptive sociology to begin with the environment and then trace its effects upon the occupations of a people, upon their sociology, and so forth. The method is a suggestive one, and has led to brilliant generalizations. The danger consists of theorizing from imperfect data, and the influence of alien cultures is largely ignored.

Professor Karl Ritter (1779-1859) of Berlin published between 1822 and 1859 the nineteen volumes of *Die Erdkunde im Verhaltniss zur Natur und zur Geschichte des Menschen.* These works formed the basis from which was developed the German view of geography as a science of the correlation of distributions. In 1859 T. Waitz (1821-64), in his *Anthropologie der Naturvölker,* insisted on the inter-relation between physical conditions and the psychic life of mankind. Amongst others who were exponents of this line of thought were A. von Humboldt, Herder, Cotta, and Kohl, and later Peschel, Kirchhoff, Bastian, and G. Gerland (1833-1919) (in Waitz); but the greatest of these was Friedrich Ratzel (1844-1904), who placed anthropogeography on a scientific basis in his standard work.[11]

In his *History of Civilization* (1857-1861), T. Buckle (1821-1862) asks the question "Are the actions of men, and therefore of societies, governed by fixed laws, or are they the result either of chance or supernatural interference?" He attempted to show how environment was the dominant influence in early societies, but he tried to prove too much. This theme ruins through Payne's *History of the New World called America,* and J.W. Draper's (1811-1882) *History of the Intellectual Development of Europe* (1861).

Ellsworth Huntingdon[12] has written numerous books and papers dealing with the effects of environment on mankind. Other writers are: A.J. Herbertson and F.D. Herbertson,[13] who wrote a valuable small book based on the Le Play method. The work of J. Brunhes[14] deserves especial mention. In an ingenious paper,[15] W.D. Mathew argues that all groups of mammals arose within, and dispersed progressively in process of time from, the centre of Asia, and claims "that the environment in which man primarily evolved! was not a moist or tropical climate, but a temperate and even more or less arid one, progressively cold and dry during the course of his evolution" (p. 212). H. Bryn[16] discusses the racial history of Asia from a geographical point of view in a very interesting manner.

The "migration-zone theory of race evolution" of Griffith Taylor is given in his brilliant and provocative book,[17] but it has not been accepted by ethnologists.

Since about the middle of the last century various branches of ethnology have been studied in a comparative manner, and mainly from the evolutionary point of view.

Sir Edward Tylor (1832-1917) was the conoured and best-known exponent of comparative ethnology, and his two great works,[18] while replete with immense erudition, are so suggestive and charmingly written that they profoundly influenced contemporary thought. Some idea of the magnitude and diversity of his work (published between 1861 and 1907) may be gathered from the bibliography collected by Miss B. Freire-Marreco.[19]

A further stimulus in this country to the study of various aspects of ethnology was given by Sir John Lubbock (Lord Avebury) (1834-1913),[20] who interested a large public, as also did Edward Clodd (1840-1930).[21]

Folklore is essentially the study of survivals of more primitive conditions in civilized communities, most of which persist because they still have a functional value. The term "folklore" was coined in 1846[22] by W.J. Thomas ("Ambrose Merton"), a founder of the Folklore Society, and that of "survivals" was first employed by Tylor;[23] Sir G. Laurence Gomme (1853-1916) devoted much time to the historical, sociological, and ethnological interpretation of folklore, and he especially recognized the importance of method, and endeavoured to raise folklore to a scientific status. He wrote: Not only is it necessary to ascertain the proper position of each item of folklore in the culture area in which it is found, but it is also necessary to ascertain its scientific relationships to other items found in the same area; and I have protested against the too easy attempt to proceed upon the comparative method. Before we can compare we must be certain that we are comparing like quantities."[24] A comparison of the aims and methods of Tylor and Gomme is given by R.R. Marett.[25]

At the Folk-Lore Congress held in London in 1891[26] there was a discussion on the independent origin of folk-tales *versus* their transmission. The evolutionists tended to minimize the evidence for borrowing, but E.S. Hartland pointed out that: "The anthropological theory of folk-tales no more excludes the possibility of multitudes of instances of dissemination than the anthropological theory of civilization." Those with a literary bias paid more attention to each tale as a whole, and justly argued that, whereas certain details might occur spontaneously, a complex could not do so, and however wide the distribution of a connected series of incidents in a tale might be, it could be accounted for only by dissemination. The publication in 1893 of the variants of the tale of *Cinderella,* by Miss M.E. Roalfe Cox (1860-1916), gave occasion for the discussion to break out anew.[27] Joseph Jacobs pointed out that: "The survivals found in folk-tales or custom cannot be used as evidence of the former existence of the beliefs on which those survivals are founded in the actual place where either tale or custom is now to be met with, since the primitive savage characters in folk-tales may have been introduced into a country when they had already arrived at the stage of survivals."[28]

Being impressed by the gradual improvement in firearms, and believing that the same principles of evolution must govern the development of the other arts, appliances, and ideas of mankind, Colonel Lane Fox [A. Lane-Fox Pitt-Rivers (1827-1900)] began in 1851 to make the famous ethnological collection which is now in the University Museum of Oxford and bears his name. His first paper was published in 1867, and it and subsequent lectures are reprinted in *The Evolution of Culture and other Essays,* 1906. The collections have been arranged and augmented by Henry Balfour, who has written many papers on the evolution, distribution, and diffusion of various arts and crafts.[29] Among the few who followed the line of research initiated by Lane Fox was Miss A.W. Buckland,[30] but the biological conception of evolution was so dominant among students that the historical aspects of ethnology were largely inhibited. As we have seen, the study of folklore was similarly affected.

Dr. H.S. Harrison, in the interests of the clear thinking that is essential to the solution of the problems connected with the history of invention and with the diffusion of culture, sought to give precision to the terms "discovery" and "invention."[31] R.U. Sayce[32] has written an introduction to the study of material culture which, with scientific detachment, deals with general principles and the problems of invention and diffusion in an admirable manner.

Otis T. Mason (1838-1908), of the United States National Museum, paid particular attention to the implements and processes of the technology of backward peoples.[33]

There is still discussion concerning the frequency of the independent invention of objects or processes. As a matter of fact, it is extremely difficult to give unequivocal examples of these, as was recognized by F. von Luschan (1854-1924)[34] in 1918.

Pitt-Rivers was perhaps the first to suggest that patterns and designs may be studied from an evolutionary point of view. The first systematic treatise on this subject was by Dr. Colley March, who in "The Meaning of Ornament"[35] utilized certain views put forward by G. Semper in *Der Stil* (1860-63), but for over a decade Dr. Hjalmar Stolpe (1841-1905) had been collecting material on these lines; he published a memoir on Polynesian art in 1890 and one on American art in 1896.[36] C.H. Read,[37] H. Balfour,[38] and numerous American (W.H. Holmes, F. Boas etc.) and German (Verworn, von den Steinen, K.T. Preuss etc.) ethnologists have studied the decorative art of various regions. A.C. Hadldon[39] first drew attention to the value of form, technique, and motif of decorative art, combined with ethnographical data, in the delimitation of definite cultural areas.

That the similarity of cultural phenomena in different places is explainable by migration or borrowing was held to a slight extent by Morgan, Bastian, and Tylor, but the fructification of this line of study was due to F. Ratzel,[40] who stated that there was no necessary spatial limit to the migration or borrowing of cultural objects or of whole complexes. L. Frobenius extended Ratzel's idea, and called his own method "geographical-statistical." F. Graebner also broke away from the sterilizing influence of Bastian's "Elementargedanke" and followed the method of Ratzel. In 1905 he published a memorable paper, "Kulturkreise und Kulturschichten in Ozeanien," *Zeits. f. Ethnol.* XXXVII, p. 28, and A. Ankermann a similar one on Africa (p. 54). Graebner followed this with "Die Melanesische Bogenkultur und ihre Verwandten," *Anthropos,* IV, 1909, pp. 726, 998, and W. Schmidt essayed the same procedure for South America, *Zeits. f. Ethnol.,* XLV, 1913, p. 1014. W. Foy and J. Lips are also adherents of this school. Graebner rejected the evolutionary theory (and also to a large extent convergence) in ethnology, and stated that similar invention in different places is so very rare that it can be assumed only when a common historical origin cannot be traced. Therefore, the task of ethnology, as he understood it, becomes the reconstruction of separate migrations each with a special complex of cultural traits. His method consists of mapping the distribution of cultures and objects, and the approximate coincidence of distributions is held to indicate a definite historical association. This method is largely a mechanical one, as there is no necessary functional connection between the several elements of a complex. These hypothetical culture-waves and areas are so speculative that the "culture-historical school" has been severely criticized by German and American[41] ethnologists. Rivers,[42] on the other hand, adopted the principle of building up his cultures on elements which were inter-related functionally.

Graebner published later a monograph of his hypothetical Bow-culture, and in 1911 his *Methode der Ethnologie,* the first book on the subject; here ethnology is treated as more allied to history than to the natural sciences. As an endeavour to methodize ethnology, the book is of value, though open to correction on many points. In a review of it, Pater W. Schmidt states[43] that ethnological evolutionism will never recover from Graebner's relentless criticism, and he subscribes to all that is said by Graebner about McLenhan, Morgan, Tylor, Breysig, and other evolutionists, and finishes by asserting that the method formulated by Graebner is the most important during the past fifty years in the history of ethnology.

Principal Dr. W. Robertson of Edinburgh, who was influenced by Cartesian scholasticism and followed the teaching of Fontenelle, who himself was completely dominated by the *a priori* method of Descartes, says in *The History of America,* 1777: "The disposition and manners of men are formed by their situation, and arise from the state of society in which they live.... There is nothing wonderful, then, in the similitude between the Americans and the barbarous nations of our continent."[44] This line of thought was definitely formulated by Bastian (p. 64).

In 1750 Turgot applied the Newtonian method in science to the study of mankind; he wrote: "All epochs are fastened together by a sequence of causes and effects, linking the condition of the world to all the conditions that have gone before it."[45] If the historical method had been strictly followed, many hypotheses would have received a different exposition, and ethnology would have a better claim to be recognised as a scientific study.

Dr. E.B. Tylor acknowledges that he attempts "to sketch a theoretical course of civilization among mankind," which he terms a "progression-theory of civilization," but admits that "culture gained by progression may be lost by degradation," and adds, "Civilization is a plant much oftener propagated than developed."[46]

In the United States, as in this country, the earlier anthropologists, such as L.H. Morgan, Major Powell, O.T. Mason, D.G. Brinton, and others, were under the spell of evolution. For the past fifty years American ethnologists, as was natural and proper, have accumulated a vast mass of all kinds of anthropological material from their own country, which was mainly uncorrelated till Franz Boas studied the material and trained students in strict method and critical approach; an outstanding linguist himself, he emphasized the importance of linguistics and philology. Boas soon became the leader and inspirer of American ethnologists, and he imbued them with his scientific spirit and his appreciation of the historical and psychological points of view.

When working out the ethnographic collections in the American Museum of Natural History, Boas found that the continent of North America could be divided into districts, or culture-areas, each characterized by a more or less distinct material culture. He and his disciples concentrated research upon districts restricted both historically and in their geographical extensions, and also upon the psychology of the association, inter-penetration, and assimilation of cultural traits. Boas introduced the concept of "pattern" in the description of tribal or area cultures; he rejected evolution and environmentalism in their crude classical forms and accepted diffusion, independent development, parallelism, and convergence, not as dogmatic postulates but as tools to aid research.[47]

The problems of convergence and parallelism are discussed by Goldenweiser, who says (p. 50):

> Since the time of Spencer, Tylor, and Frazer the resemblance of cultural traits in different cultural complexes[48] have become commonplaces in ethnology. The orthodox evolutionist correlated these similarities with parallel series of developments rooted ultimately in the psychic unity of man. The results of historical and ethnological research proved fatal to this conception.... The rigorous application of the psychological point of view led to similar conclusions.... [but] a wide domain of genuine cultural similarities survived the onslaught of critical analysis. Thus arose a peculiar situation: similarities in cultural traits had to be correlated with diversities in historical processes. The principle of convergence seems admirably fitted for this task.

It is necessary to point out that the academic conception of the "pattern" of the behaviour of a social group has often been unduly stressed, while the numerous and significant exceptions have received little attention or have been ignored.

"The Geographical Distribution Theory," as it has been termed in America, is similar to the "Age and Area" theory of naturalists; its first application in anthropology was made by N.C. Nelson in 1919,[49] and has been elaborated by Clark Wissler.

Broadly speaking, it is found that when in each area there is a concentric zonal distribution of a culture trait-complex, the zones can safely be interpreted as superpositions, and from these time relations can be assumed; it may also be inferred that basic or undifferentiated distributions took longer to develop and run their courses than the later and more specialized. The cultural layers are like horizontal strata which had increasingly smaller areas as time progressed, and thus a sort of step-pyramid diagram can be constructed. The same applies to America as a whole. The more specialized traits occur approximately towards the centre of a culture area, not the traits widely distributed over the continent, which indicates that there has been an adjustment to some particular environment, and thus these traits came to be specialized. "Traits from living tribes do centre in the hearts of culture areas" (p. 216), but exceptions occur for the distributions of archaeological artifacts. "The principle of concentric distribution is an ecological phenomenon...it is in the nucleus of the ecological centre that a type of aboriginal culture is at its best" (p. 219). The centres of distribution revealed by archaeology in unexpected places may" be explained by the ecology of those particular periods. Human traits have definite distributions because they are adjusted to external conditions. The foregoing bald summary is taken from Clark Wissler's *The Relation of Nature to Man in Aboriginal America,* 1926; the culture areas are defined in his *The American Indian,* 1917. A.L. Kroeber, in his *Anthropology,* 1923, gives (p. 340) a diagrammatic representation of accumulation and diffusion of culture traits. In his thesis *The Chronological Aspects of Certain Australian Social Institutions as Inferred from Geographical Distribution,* Philadelphia, 1928, D.S. Davidson made an interesting, but unconvincing, application of this method to Australia. Graebner, Schmidt, and Rivers recognize the complexity of Australian culture, but account for it in different ways.

The diffusion of cultures, or of various elements of culture, in the Old World, despite notable discontinuous distributions, has not presented the same difficulty of interpretation as has been felt for the cultural similarities between the New and the Old World. Some of them were referred to by Principal W. Robertson of Edinburgh in his *The History of America,* 1777, but only to be dismissed as "so equivocal, that no theory...ought to be founded upon them." Baron A. von Humboldt (1769-1859)[50] stated a definite case for the derivation of American culture from eastern Asia and India, but Lord Kingsborough[51] poured scorn on this idea. W.H. Prescott, in *The Conquest of Mexico,* 1843, played with the possibility of a positive communication between the hemispheres, but he could not make up his mind on the subject. Gustave d'Eichthal argued in favour of the Buddhist origin of the American civilization.[52] E.B. Tylor[53] produced similar evidence, and elsewhere has given many examples of Asiatic and American cultural similarities.[54] The foregoing summary is taken from Elliot Smith's *The Diffusion of Culture,* 1933, who says (p. 139): "The evidence collected by Humboldt, d'Eichthal, Tylor, and many others, establishes the fact that the early civilisation of America, its pyramids [etc.]... are thoroughly Indian, or rather Indo-Chinese, in motive and feeling." But Tylor reverted to the old evolutionary doctrine and stated that: "American man, for example, need not necessarily owe the minutest portion of his mental, religious, social, or industrial development to remote contact with Asia or Europe, though he were proved to possess identical usages."[55] American ethnologists as a whole deny the transmission of cultural traits from Asia to America, but G. Friederici is convinced that this took place.[56] Elliot Smith goes so far as to say that "many thousands of boatloads of immigrants must have arrived on the Pacific coast of America, bringing with them a variety of contributions from the civilisations of the Old World."[57] R.B. Dixon[58] says: "But although Polynesians did thus very rarely, and probably at long intervals, make such contacts with the people of South America, the net result was negligible so far as America as a whole or South America in particular was concerned."

Elliot Smith asserts that "the principle of diffusion explains" why "the civilisation of the whole world was derived from one original source" (p. 232) and says: "The evidence which is now available justifies the inference that civilisation originated in Egypt, perhaps as early as 4000 B.C., but certainly before 3500 B.C." (p. 222) and says: "It is no exaggeration to claim that the arts and crafts, the social and political organization, and the innermost beliefs and the symbolism of the whole world were largely shaped by the practice of embalming" (p. 216).

Fig. 9.2: G. Elliot Smith

When Dr. G. Elliot Smith was Professor of Anatomy in the University of Cairo, he investigated royal and other mummies; this led him to inquire into the significance of mummification, and thence to funeral monuments and the numerous aspects of the early Egyptian funeral customs, and his range has been widening ever since. In 1915 he published *The Migrations of Early Culture,* but since 1911 he has published numerous books and papers on various subjects, in which he ardently advocates his thesis. Early he secured the loyal support of Dr. W.J. Perry, who, in his courageous book *The Children of the Sun,* 1923, elaborated the doctrine that civilization in its essentials arose only in Egypt, and with some secondary accretions spread throughout the whole world, losing some of its heterogeneous elements as it spread, but retaining the majority, so that, the peculiar character of the culture can be clearly traced. This spread was originally and correctly termed a "Migration" by Elliot Smith, but later he adopted the term "the

Diffusion of Culture"; the agents who disseminated the "Archaic Culture" (originally called the "Heliolithic Culture-Complex") are termed "the Children of the Sun," and the lures which enticed them onward in their migrations have been duly enumerated by Perry. This propaganda has been supported by some enthusiastic adherents in England, whose writings are referred to in the publications of Elliot Smith and Perry. Professor Roland B. Dixon of Harvard University criticized this theory in *The Building of Culture,* 1928, and American ethnologists, in particular, are sceptical. Long ago, Gerland postulated the persistence of a number of cultural traits which were developed in one centre and carried by man in his migrations from continent to continent.

When Dr. W.H.R. Rivers (1864-1922) began his monumental work *The History of Melanesian Society,* 1914, he was, as he pointed out in his Address,[59] under the dominance of the evolutionary theory, but when he came to analyse Melanesian society, he realized the influence exerted by relatively small bodies of immigrants upon the older cultures, and that the social adjustments superficially resembled what might easily be regarded as evolutionary processes. On the other hand, when the contact of cultures takes place, new features often appear, and the contact supplies the dynamic element for evolutionary change. In 1915 and 1916[60] and in 1922[61] he confesses his adherence to the views of Elliot Smith and Perry.

Huxley said it is the customary fate of new truths to begin as heresies and end as superstitions. Everyone can endorse the appeal made to the student of human institutions by Elliot Smith: "It is not a matter of vital significance whether he accepts or rejects these interpretations of the evidence. But it is a matter of fundamental importance that he should repeatedly submit to impartial and critical examination the evidence upon which his theories are built up, and that, whatever view he adopts, it should be founded upon unquestionable data and strictly rational arguments."[62]

In almost all regions where man is found today he has migrated from elsewhere; thus any given culture did not originate in its last home: this merely modified the culture already acquired in its manifold migrations. In these migrations were encountered not only different environments, but also different peoples, each with its special culture, all of which more or less affected the culture in question. The historical method endeavours to unravel this tangle. As Pater W. Schmidt points out, "the historical method does not see any obstacle in the way of establishing such relations... over great distances and in the cases of discontinuous diffusion, because we are absolutely sure that migrations from great distances really took place in innumerable instances though no connecting links now exist."[63]

Professor A.R. Radcliffe-Brown[64] says:

> It is impossible to reconcile the different theories with one another, or even to discover principles of method about which there is general agreement. To say nothing of theories of the derivation of culture from a lost Atlantis or a lost Pacific continent, we are offered a choice between the Egyptian theory championed in its latest form by Prof. Elliot Smith, or the theory of culture-cycles of Graebner, or the somewhat different theory of Father Schmidt, or that of Frobenius, and I know not how many more. Each school goes its own way, building up its own hypothetical structure, not attempting to seek out points on which agreement can be reached with others. The procedure is often that of disciples of a cult rather than that of students of a science (p. 148).

Speaking for American anthropologists, Boas says:

> The method which we try to develop is based on a study of the dynamic changes in society that may be observed at the present time. We refrain from the attempt to solve the

> fundamental problem of the general development of civilization until we have been able to unravel the processes that are going on under our eyes.[65]

A consideration of the ethnological publications of the last forty years will show that they fall into three main groups: (1) ethnographical accounts of actual fieldwork; (2) those that are the product of researches in libraries or museums; (3) those in which the fieldworker also makes use of comparative studies, which preferably are drawn from neighbouring fields.

The method of treatment of ethnographical studies is undergoing a change. Usually the data of economic, social, and religious life have been described as almost independent phenomena, with the result that they presented static pictures, which, even when combined, were insufficient to form a true panorama of life, and they did not sufficiently present those interacting activities and motives that alone can give rise to a satisfying conception of a living society.

It was his experience in the field combined with theoretical knowledge that led Professor B. Malinowski to formulate in 1926 his "functional method". This method is explained and illustrated by his *Argonauts of the Western Pacific* (1922). In this book he describes a peculiar system termed *kula* in the archipelagoes off South-east New Guinea, which establishes a relation between magic, mythology, social organization, purely commercial interests, and a half-ceremonial half-aesthetic system of values built round objects whose primary function was adornment, but which soon became simply repositories of a traditional and competitive principle of value. The same method is employed in his *The Sexual Life of Savages* (1929; 3rd ed. with a foreword on method, 1932). Belonging to this school are Raymond Firth,[66] who first dealt with primitive economics from the functional point of view, and Audrey I. Richards, who did the same for food.[67]

Margaret Mead was working on similar lines,[68] and another good example of the "functional method" was written by R.F. Fortune;[69] but this method has been implicit in the best ethnographical works, as, for example, in the two volumes of H.A. Junod's *The Life of a South African Tribe,* 1912, 1913. E.T. Torday says:[70] "The idea of functional anthropology is not absolutely new. It may be said to have been applied, so far as Africa is concerned, by Dapper in his *Accurate Description of African Regions* etc., published in Amsterdam in 1668. In more enlightened days he would have founded a school of functional anthropology."

Notes

1. *Lucretius, On the Nature of Things [de rerum natura].* Translated by H.A.J. Munro. Bohn's Classical Library, 1908, p. 214.
2. E.H. Man, *J.A.I., XV,* p. 442.
3. Père Lafitau: *Mœurs des sauvages américans comparées aux mœurs des premiers temps,* Paris, 1729. He regarded primitive peoples as living witnesses of stages in the history of humanity. In this he was followed by Jens Kraft, a Danish Professor of philosophy, *Die Sitten der Wilden. Zur Aufklärung des Ursprungs der Menschheit* (Kopenhagen, 1766).
4. *Buckle and his Critics*, 1895, p. 7.
5. *De la République*, 1576; *Of the Lawes and Customes of a Common Wealth,* Eng. ed., 1605.
6. *Rep. Brit. Assoc,* 1909 (1910), p. 593.
7. Cf. A.H. Koller, *The Theory of Environment,* Pt. I, 1918, p. 19 (Menasha, Wisconsin).
8. *L'Esprit des Lois*, 1748.
9. R. Flint, *History of the Philosophy of History* etc., 1894. p. 279.
10. *Loc. cit.*, p. 286.
11. *Anthropogeographie* (1882-91), an adapted translation of which, *Influences of Geographic Environment*, 1911, was made by Miss E.C. Semple, who also wrote *American History and its Geographical Conditions*, 1903, and *The Geography of the Mediterranean Region*, 1931.
12. *The Pulse of Asia*, 1907; *Civilization and Climate*, 1915; *The Character of Races*, 1924, etc.
13. *Man and his Work, an Introduction to Human Geography*, 1909.
14. *La Géographie humaine,* 1910; 2nd ed., 1912.
15. "Climate and Evolution," *Ann. New York Acad. Sci.,* XXIV, I9I5, pp. 171.
16. *Ymer,* 1922, p. 314.

17. *Environment and Race,* 1927; cf. his earlier papers in the *Geographical Review,* 1919, p. 289; 1921, p. 54.
18. *Early History of Mankind*, 1865; *Primitive Culture*, 1871.
19. *Anthropological Essays presented to Edward Burnett Tylor in honour of his seventy-fifth birthday*, October 2, 1907.
20. *The Origin of Civilization and the Primitive Conditions of Man*, 1870; 6th ed., 1902.
21. *The Childhood of the World*, 1873; enlarged ed., 1914; *The Childhood of Religion*, 1875; *Tom Tit Tot*, 1898; *Animism, the Seed of Religion*, 1905; *Magic in Names and other Things*, 1920.
22. *Athenæum,* August 22, 1846.
23. *Primitive Culture*, 1871, p. 16.
24. *Folk-lore as an Historical Science*, London, 1908, p. xiii.
25. *Folk-lore,* XXVIII, 1917, pp. 13-35.
26. *The International Folk-lore Congress*, 1891, London, 1892, p. 27.
27. *Folk-lore,* IV, 1893: A. Nutt, p. 133; J. Jacobs, p. 269; A. Lang, p. 413; A. Nutt, p. 434. V, 1894: J. Jacobs, p. 129; A. Nutt, p. 146.
28. *Folk-Lore,* V, p. 140.
29. See also H. Balfour, *Rep. Brit. Assoc.*, 1904, p. 689.
30. *Journ. Anth. Inst.*, IV, 1874; XVIII, 1889; *Anthropological Studies*, London, 1891.
31. *Man,* 1926, Nos. 74, 101, 143; 1927, No. 28; "Evolution in Material Culture," *Rep. Brit. Assoc.*, 1930, p. 137; "Opportunism and the Factors of Invention," *The American Anthropologist,* XXXII, 1930, p. 106.
32. *Primitive Arts and Crafts*, Cambridge, 1933.
33. *The Origins of Inventions*, 1895; *Woman's Share in Primitive Culture*, 1895.
34. "Zusammenhänge und Konvergenz," *Mitt. d. Anthr. Ges. Wien.*, vol. 48, 1918, pp. 1-117.
35. Trans. Lane and Cheshire Ant. Soc., 1889.
36. H. Stolpe, "Utvecklingsföreteelser i naturfolkens ornamentik," *Ymer,* 1890 (translated by Mrs. H. C. March, "Evolution in the Ornamental Art of Savage Peoples," *Trans. Rochdale Lit. and Sci. Soc.*, 1891 (1892), and into German, *Mitt. Anth. Ges. Wien,* 1892, p. 43); *Studier i Amerikansk Ornamentik,* 1896.
37. *J.A.I.*, XXI, 1891, p. 139.
38. *The Evolution of Decorative Art*, 1893.
39. *The Decorative Art of British New Guinea, Cunningham Memoirs*, Roy. Irish Acad., Dublin, 1894; *Evolution in Art*, 1895.
40. *Anthropo-Geographie*, II, 1891, p. 705.
41. As for example by Roland B. Dixon, *The Building of Cultures,* 1928, p. 226, and by A. Goldenweiser, *History, Psychology, and Culture,* 1933, p. 145.
42. *The History of Melanesian Society*, 1914.
43. "Die Kulturhistorische Methode in der Ethnologie", *Anthropos,* VI, 1911, p. 1010.

44. Elliot Smith, *The Diffusion of Culture,* 1933, p. 54.
45. Elliot Smith, *loc. cit.,* p. 236.
46. *Primitive Culture,* I, 1873, pp. 21, 38, 53.
47. Cf. A. Goldenweiser, *History, Psychology, and Culture,* 1933, pp. 152 ff.
48. The term culture includes all the traits (concrete objects or abstract notions) which are possessed by a people. When traits become closely associated together and act as a unit, the grouping is known as a culture-complex, and the traits are contributory traits. A complex, however, often gives origin to other traits (derivative traits), which in time may dissociate themselves from the complex, and then diffuse independently. A contributive trait should have a distribution greater than the complex to which it has contributed, and a derivative trait should usually have a lesser distribution than the complex from which it has been derived (condensed from D.S. Davidson, 1928, pp. 8, 9).
49. "Human Culture," *Natural History,* XIX, No. 2, NewYork.
50. *Vues des Cordillères*, etc., 1813.
51. *Antiquities of Mexico,* 1831-48, VIII, p. 27.
52. *Rev. Arch. Paris*, 1865.
53. *Rep. Brit. Assoc.,* 1894, p. 774, and *Nature,* L, p. 349.
54. *Researches into the Early History of Mankind,* 1865, 1870, 1878, pp. 302, 339, but cf. p. 173; *J.A.I.,* VIII, 1878, p. 116; IX, 1879, p. 23; *Rep. Brit. Assoc.,* 1884, p. 899, and *Nature,* XXX, p. 448.
55. *Encyc. Brit,* 11th ed., 1910, Vol. II, p. 119.
56. *Mitt. aus den Deutsch. Schutzgeb.*, XXXVI, 1928, p. 27.
57. *Loc. cit.*, p. 78.
58. *The American Aborigines*, 1933, p. 353.
59. *Rep. Brit. Assoc.*, 1911, p. 490; reprinted in *Psychology and Ethnology*, 1926, p. 120.
60. *Loc. cit.*, 1926, pp. 167, 276.
61. *J.R.A.I.*, LII, p. 17.
62. "Conversion in Science," *Huxley Memorial Lectures,* 1932, p. 38.
63. *High Gods in North America*, 1933, p. 7.
64. "The Present Position of Anthropological Studies," *Rep. Brit. Assoc.*, 1931, p. 141.
65. *American Anthropologist*, XXII, 1920, p. 316.
66. *Primitive Economics of the New Zealand Maori*, 1929.
67. *Hunger and Work in a Savage Tribe: A Functional Study of Nutrition among the Southern Bantu*, 1932.
68. *Coming of Age in Samoa*, 1929; *Growing up in New Guinea* [actually the Admiralty Islands], 1930.
69. *Sorcerers of Dobu*, 1932.
70. *African Races. Descriptive Sociology,* No. 4. Compiled and abstracted upon the plan organized by Herbert Spencer, 1930. Introduction, p. i, by E.T. Torday.

Chapter X
Sociology

Sociology, as Rivers has pointed out,[1] deals with social actions which form a body of organized processes which can be described and classified. Its first business is to ascertain what happens or has happened, and then to try to explain why it happens or has happened. The final aim is the explanation of social behaviour in terms of psychology.

The word "Sociology" was first used by Auguste Comte (1798-1857), who showed that its aim was to discover the nature, the natural causes, and the natural laws of society. With the development of the natural sciences came the insistence on a naturalistic interpretation of social differences, as advocated by Guyot (1807-1884) and Draper (1811-1882) and over-emphasized by Buckle (1821-1862). Comte's method was that of deductive construction, that of Buckle is alluded to on p. 108.

The evolutionist explanation of the natural world as applied to sociology found its fullest exponent in Herbert Spencer (1820-1903), who studied the anatomy of the social frame. He derived the principles of sociology from those of psychology and of biology, and regarded social development as a super-organic evolution.

But all these earlier attempts to discover a social science were speculative. The solid foundations of inductive sociology were laid by Bachofen, Morgan, McLennan, and notably by Rivers.

J.J. Bachofen (1815-1887) (*Das Mutterrecht,* 1861) was the first to study the system of filiation through the mother, or mother-right, which was and is still widely distributed in a m6re or less developed condition. J.F. McLennan (1827-81)[2] acknowledged that this discovery was due to Bachofen, who regarded matrilineal descent as the most ancient system. He points out more than once that Maine seems not to have been able to conceive of any social order more primitive than the patrilineal. He says:

> From the time of Plato downwards, theories of human society have been current in which the family living under the headship of a father is accepted as the ultimate social unit. These theories have taken various shapes.... with Sir Henry Maine[3] the theory becomes a theory of the origin, of at least of the earliest stage of society in which Comparative Jurisprudence is called upon to take interest (1885, p. x).

McLennan was a keen controversialist, and attacked Morgan, Maine and others with unnecessary vigour and animus.

The question as to the priority of mother-right over father-right has led to much controversy. E.S. Hartland (1848-1927)[4] was a strong supporter of this view: the literature is too extensive to be noted here. At the present time this academic problem has ceased to have much interest as it has been so fully discussed.

L.H. Morgan (1818-1881) was the greatest sociologist of the past century, and in his monumental work[5] laid a solid foundation for the study of the family and kinship systems; he formulated a scheme of the evolution of the family based on a study of the classificatory system[6] of relationship, of which he was the discoverer. According to his scheme, human society has advanced, through gradual evolution, from a state of complete promiscuity to one characterized by monogamy. W.H.R. Rivers (1864-1922) points out that "in recent years the scheme has encountered much opposition.... The opponents of Morgan have made no attempt to

Fig. 10.1: W.H.R. Rivers

distinguish between different parts of his scheme, but, having shown that certain of its features are unsatisfactory, they have condemned the whole." The greater part of Morgan's work is, however, of lasting value. Morgan based his conclusions on an enormous number of kinship terms collected by himself and others from every available source. Rivers[7] developed in 1898 a new method of collecting similar data by means of recording exhaustive genealogies from a limited area. In this way not only can kinship terms be collected, but a large number of other sociological data are obtained with a readiness and accuracy not hitherto possible. It is no exaggeration to say that this method is producing a revolution in the method of sociological fieldwork, and in his hands and in those of his followers it has given rise to more scientific precision in social anthropology.[8]

In his later book Morgan summarized his earlier conclusions, and proposed a classification of culture consisting of a lower, middle, and upper Status of Savagery; a lower, middle and upper Status of Barbarism; and the Status of Civilization based upon certain inventions and industries.

About this time various students wrote on marriage and the family, among whom were Giraud-Teulon (1867, 1874, 1884), A.H. Post (1875), C. Letourneau (1888), F. von Hellwald (1889), and others, the conclusions of the earlier writers being summed up by E. Westermarck in his masterly *The History of Human Marriage* (1891, 5th ed., 1921). Among later writers are J. Kohler *(Zur Urgeschichte der Ehe,* 1897), S.A. Cook's edition (1903) of W. Robertson Smith's *Kinship and Marriage in Early Arabia* (1885), E. Crawley (1869-1924), *The Mystic Rose,* 1902, 4th ed. by T. Bestermann, 1932, and the numerous writings, of W.H.R. Rivers, already referred to.

Tylor[9] endeavoured "to show that the development of institutions may be investigated on a basis of tabulation and classification." This method was applied to "Laws of Marriage and Descent," but it has not been adopted by others, as its value depends upon the units of comparison being of equivalent value, which it is difficult to ensure.

In a suggestive book[10] A. van Gennep has shown that almost universally there is a general, similarity between the character and the sequence of the rites concerned with the great events of life—initiation, marriage, death, and the like. These are: (1) rites of separation, that mark the severance from the previous condition; (2) transitional or marginal rites; and (3) rites of admission, which are concerned with integration into a new status. This generalization has had a considerable influence among fieldworkers and others.

The various types of social and religious groupings form a fascinating study about which a great deal has been written by fieldworkers and systematists, of which two may be mentioned.[11]

A.M. Hocart[12] has published an interesting book on the important subject of kingship, on which Sir James Frazer[13] has also written.

Magic and religion are very generally held to be not only distinct from one another, but also antithetical. There is now a tendency to regard them as originally analogous phenomena, both being expressions of a belief in a power or energy, "mana," "orenda," etc., which is tapped directly by "magical" practices; but, when it is exercised by spirits, "religious" practices are employed. In some cases it is difficult, perhaps impossible, to determine whether certain actions can be classed as either magical or religious, as they appear to belong to both categories.

The comparative study of magic has to some extent been undertaken by Frazer, A.B. Jevons,[14] and others; but one of the most important contributions to the subject is by Hubert and Mauss[15] who treat it from a sociological aspect.

Parson Thwackum in *Tom Jones* says: "When I mention religion I mean the Christian religion; and not only the Christian religion, but the Protestant religion; and not only the Protestant religion, but the Church of England." Anthropology, by a reverse process, passes, "in larger sympathy from specific creeds to partake of the universal spirit which every creed tries to embody."[16] The interest of anthropology in religion was defined by Huxley:[17] "Anthropology has nothing to do with the truth or falsehood of religion—it holds itself absolutely and entirely aloof from such questions—but the natural history of religion, and the origin and growth of the religions entertained by the different kinds of the human race, are within its proper and legitimate province."

This is not the place to attempt a definition of religion—a task which has led to so many failures. We must be content with the statement that it most frequently presents itself under the aspects of ritual, myth, and belief. Ethnologists have hitherto practically confined their attention to ritual and myth, and but too frequently exclusively to the latter.

As Andrew Lang[18] (1844-1912) points out, in the sixth century B.C. Xenophanes complained that the gods were credited with the worst crimes, and other classical writers were shocked at the contradictions between the conception and ritual worship of the same god. In ancient Egypt the priests strove to strip the burden of absurdity and sacrilege from their own deities. It taxed the ingenuity of pious Brahmans to explain the myths which made Indra the slayer of the three-headed Visvarupa (p. 15). Euhemerus (316 B.C.), in his philosophical romance, *Sacra Historica,* in rationalizing the fables about the gods, was regarded as an atheist. Certain writers like Plutarch (A.D. 60) and Porphyry (A.D. 270) made the ancient deities types of their own favourite doctrines, whatever these might happen to be. The early Christians had a good case against the heathen. Eusebius, in the *Proeparatio Evangelica,* anticipating Andrew Lang himself, " ridicules, with a good deal of humour, the old theories which resolved so many mythical heroes into the sun" (p. 20). "The physical interpreters," said Eusebius, "do not even agree in their physical interpretations." The light of the anthropological method had dawned on Eusebius. Many centuries later, Spencer, Master of Corpus Christi College, Cambridge (1630-1693), had no other scheme in his mind in his erudite work on Hebrew ritual[19] which he considered was but an expurgated adaptation of heathen customs. Fontenelle[20] explains the irrational element in myth as inherited from savagery.

The revival of learning made scholars acquainted with the religions of Greece and Rome and of those of the nations with whom the Greeks and Romans had come in contact—Egyptians, Semites, Persians, and Indians. Travellers gave accounts of the religions they found in remote parts of the world, and missionaries reported on beliefs and customs of many nations. These were the sources from which were compiled the comprehensive works on religion from Alexander Ross, *View of All the Religions in the World,* etc., 1652, to C.F. Dupuis (1742-1809), *Origines de tous les cultes ou Religion Universelle,* 1794. All heathen religions were believed to be based on sun and star worship.

New vistas were opened up by the writings of de Brosses,[21] who investigated the beliefs of savage races and based all religion on " Fetishism".

To quote once more from Lang:

> In the beginning of the [nineteenth] century Germany turned her attention to mythology. In a pious kind of spirit, Friedrich Creuzer (1771-1858) sought to find *symbols* of some pure, early, and Oriental theosophy in the myths and mysteries of Greece.... The great Lobeck, in his *Aglaophamus* (1829), brought back common sense, and made it the guide of his vast his unequalled learning. In a gentler and more genial spirit, C., Ottfried Müller (1797-1840) laid the foundation of a truly scientific and historical mythology.[22] Neither of these writers had, like Alfred Maury,[23] much knowledge of the myths and faiths of the lower races, but they often seem on the point of anticipating the ethnological method.[24]

The study of the myths of various peoples is receiving the attention of numerous students; in Germany certain ethnologists, such as Ehrenreich, Foy,[25] and Frobenius[26] find sun and moon-gods in many unexpected places.

The collections of Märchen (1812-13) of the brothers Grimm[27] contained Teutonic myths, and by their resemblance to Norse, Greek, and Vedic mythology suggested that in German folklore were remains of a common Indo-European tradition. This was the beginning of the intelligent study of folklore. Mannhardt (1865) and his numerous followers investigated present customs and beliefs connected with agriculture and vegetation, and showed that here, in what Christianity had reduced to "superstition," were to be found survivals of the religions that Christianity had supplanted. A memorable study of tradition in story, custom, and belief is *The Legend of Perseus,* 1894, by E.S. Hartland.

Meanwhile the anthropological signification of religion was emerging from the mass of materials collected from all over the globe; these established its universality, and many attempts were made to find a common factor, first in astral worship, then in

Euhemerism (Banier, 1738), Fetishism (de Brosses, 1709-77), Nature-worship (Max Müller etc.), Ancestor-worship [Herbert Spencer, Lippert (1866) etc.], Animism (Tylor), Totemism, and so forth. The lowest existing religions can hardly be expected to inform us what was the beginning of religion when we realize that the least advanced savages are separated by as many generations from the beginnings of religion as ourselves. Further, during this enormous period of time there has been constant change, growth, borrowing, and decay—and decay is not a simple return to the primal state.

The study of comparative religion, though not originated by Max Müller (1823-1900), owed much of its popularity to his energy. His *Lectures on Comparative Mythology* (1856) were followed by *Lectures on the Science of Religion* (1870), and *Introduction to the Science of Religion* (1873). His *Contributions to the Science of Mythology* appeared in 1897. His method of investigation was almost entirely linguistic, based on phonetic laws which later research has discredited; and his theory of "mythology as the disease of language" is no longer tenable. The hymns of the Rig Veda are by no means the product of a simple society, as he supposed; in his view hymns and myths were dissociated from ritual religion, and gods were identified with natural objects. The death-blow in our country to this method of studying religion was given by the keen criticism of Andrew Lang[28]. The silly senseless, and savage element in classical mythology proved to be the stumbling block over which Max Müller fell.

In his classic work, *Primitive Culture,* 1871, E.B. Tylor marshalled his mass of evidence with balanced judgment and lucidity of style, and elaborated his famous theory of Animism which long held the field. Animism was defined as "the belief in the existence of Spiritual Beings," and was regarded as a basis common to all religions. The theory was adopted with modifications by Herbert Spencer, but was rejected by Durkheim, and Elliot Smith terms it a "dying doctrine" (1933, p. 178).

Dr. R.R. Marett, who approaches religious problem from a psychological point of view, regards Supernaturalism as a basic feeling which may well be prior to Animism; he defines it as composed of fear, admiration, wonder, and the like, which may be expressed as "awe". This can be experienced in relation with animate or inanimate objects, and he termed it Pre-animistic Religion, which is fundamentally a mode of social behaviour.[29] The attribution of personality to departments of physical nature (but not of soul or spirit) he terms Animatism. He regards "tabu" as the negative and "mana," which may be briefly described as power, as the positive mode of the supernatural. Tabu is prohibitive or even threatening, whereas mana is operative and wonder-working. Pre-animistic religion would in this case seem to be the substratum out of which definite magic and definite religion might have differentiated. What Marett terms "awe" is designated by Goldenweiser as "thrill," and he states that ultimately magic divested itself completely of the religious thrill.[30]

The nature and problems of totemism have played a great part in ethnological literature; sometimes its social significance has been emphasized, at other times its religious aspects; Goldenweiser defines it as " the specific socialization of emotional values." Nearly every writer on the subject expresses different views from those of other writers, but scarcely one of them has any original facts to offer. Certain ethnologists accept the view that different forms of totemism arose independently, and regard each variety as part of a more extensive system of beliefs and customs. The most prolific writers in this country on totemism are A. Lang[31] and Frazer, who published a little book, *Totemism,* in 1887 and in 1910 four large volumes, *Totemism and Exogamy,* in which he "summarizes all the available data with his customary skill. Róheim's *Australian Totemism* is alluded to on p. 65. E. Durkheim (1858-1917)[32] has given a brilliant psychological analysis of religious consciousness based on Australian totemism, in which, assuming it to be a religion, he finds the germs of the more elaborate religions. Goldenweiser[33] has made an extensive analytical study of totemism, in which he criticizes the views held by numerous writers, including Durkheim's theory of the origin and nature of religion.

Some students make intensive studies of particular forms of religion, either historical, such as *The Religion of the Semites* (1889; revised ed. by S.A. Cook, 1927), by Robertson Smith (1846-1894), and *The Cults of the Greek States* (1896-1909) and *Hero Cults* (1921), by L.R. Farnell (1856-1934), or of living peoples by missionaries and field workers which are too numerous to specify. Other writers attempt, by correlating the mass of material, to discover fundamental religious conceptions and to trace some of their developments.

In *The Making of Religion* (1898, 2nd ed., 1900) Andrew Lang maintained the "hypothesis of an early Supreme Being among savages, obscured later by ancestor-worship and ghost-gods," and to this extent was opposed to the evolutionary doctrine of that period. Pater W. Schmidt adopted Lang's thesis and has written largely upon "High Gods."[34] Schmidt claims that definite evidence is now available to prove that "these High Gods, in their oldest form, come before all other elements of religion, be they naturism, fetishism, ghost-worship, animism, totemism, or magism, from one or other of which the earlier evolutionistic theories had derived the origin of religion."[35]

To those who are acquainted with the modern study of comparative religion in this country it is unnecessary to point out the influence of such workers as Mannhardt, Tylor, and Robertson Smith on subsequent writers; nor is it needful to draw attention to the vast erudition and eloquent writings of Sir James G. Frazer: *The Belief in Immortality and the Worship of the Dead,* 1913; *Folk-lore in the Old Testament,* 1918; *The Worship of Nature,* 1926; and the monumental series of *The Golden Bough,* not to mention his other books.

The origin of moral ideas has in this country been discussed from the ethnological point of view by L.T. Hobhouse, *Morals in*

Evolution, 1906, and E. Westermarck, *The Origin and Development of the Moral Ideas,* 1906.

Magic, religion, and morality have been regarded in recent times almost entirely from the evolutionary point of view, a method of approach which is very different from that of Durkheim, Hubert and Mauss, Malinowski, and others, who maintain that these are essentially social phenomena and function as such.

Notes

1. *Sociological Rev.*, 1916, and *Psychology and Ethnology*, 1926.
2. *Primitive Marriage*, 1865; 2nd ed., 1876; *Studies in Ancient History*, 1876; *The Patriarchal Theory*, 1885; *Studies in Ancient History*, the Second Series, 1896.
3. *Ancient Law*, 1861.
4. *Primitive Paternity*, 1909.
5. "Systems of Consanguinity and Affinity of the Human Family," *Smithsonian Contributions to Knowledge,* Vol. XVII, 1871; *Ancient Society,* 1878.
6. In the classificatory system many of the kin in the same generation are grouped under one general term; *e.g.* all the males of the grandfather's generation are called by one term; another term includes father, father's brothers, father's male cousins, mother's sisters' husbands, mother's female cousins' husbands; and so on.
7. "A Genealogical Method of Collecting Social and Vital Statistics," *J.A.I.*, XXX, 1900, p. 74. "On the Origin of the Classificatory System of Relationships," *Anthropological Essays* (Tylor Volume), 1907, p. 309. *Reports of the Camb. Anth. Exped. to Torres Straits,* V, 1904; VI, 1908; *The Todas,* 1906; *Kinship and Social Organization,* 1914; *The History of Melanesian Society,* 1914.
8. The "Remarks on Genealogy in Connection with Anthropology" *(Mem. Anth. Soc.,* II, 1866, p. 68), by G.W. Marshall, fell on deaf ears.
9. *Journ. Anth. Inst.,* XVIII, 1889, p. 245.
10. *Les Rites de Passage*, 1909.
11. H. Schurtz, *Altersklassen und Männerbünde,* 1902 (who erroneously includes the Australian matrimonial classes with age-grades). Hutton Webster, *Primitive Secret Societies,* 1908.
12. *Kingship*, 1927.
13. *Lectures on the Early History of the Kingship,* 1905.
14. *An Introduction to the History of Religion*, 1896, 1902.
15. H. Hubert et M. Mauss, "Esquisse d'une théorie générate de la magie," *L'Ann. sociol.,* VII, 1904. M. Mauss, "L'Origine des pouvoirs magiques

dans les sociétés Australiennes," *École pratique des Hautes Études sec. relig.*, 1904.

16. Clodd, *Animism*, 1905, p. 11.
17. *Rep. Brit. Assoc.*, 1878, p. 575.
18. *Myth, Ritual, and Religion* (1887), 1899 ed. I, pp. 6, 7.
19. *De Legibus Hebraeorum Ritualibus*, 1732.
20. "De l'Origine des Fables": *Oevres*, Vol. III, 1758.
21. *Dieux fétiches*, 1760.
22. *Introduction to a Scientific System of Mythology*, English trans., London, 1844.
23. *Histoire des Religions de la Grèce Antique*, Paris, 1857.
24. *Loc. cit.*, p. 23.
25. *Archiv für Religionswissenschaft*, X, 1907, etc.
26. "Die Weltanschauung der Naturvölker, *Beitr. z. Volksund Völkerkunde*, VI, 1898; *Das Zeitalter des Sonnengottes*, I, 1904; The Childhood of Man, 1909.
27. *J.K.L.*, 1785-1863; W.K., 1786-1859.
28. *Custom and Myth*, 1884, new ed., 1899; *Myth, Ritual, and Religion*, 1887.
29. *Folk-Lore*, 1900, p. 162; reprinted in his valuable book *The Threshold of Religion*, 1909.
30. *History, Psychology, and Culture*, p. 383.
31. Social Origins, 1903; *The Secret of the Totem*, 1905.
32. *Les formes élémentaires de la vie religieuse; le système totemique en Australie*, 1912; trs. by G. W. Swain, *The Elementary Forms of the Religious Life*, 1915.
33. *Totemism: An Analytical Study*, 1910; *History, Psychology, and Culture*, 1933.
34. "L'Origine de l'idee de Dieu," *Anthropos*, 1908-10; and *Der Ursprung der Gottesidee*, Münster i. W., 1912; enlarged ed., 1926.
35. W. Schmidt, *High Gods in North America*, Oxford, 1933, p. 3.

References

Allen, Grant. *The Evolution of the Idea of God*, London, 1897.

Bastian, A. *Die Vorgeschichte der Ethnologie*, Berlin, 1881.

British Museum Handbook to the Ethnographical Collections, London, 1910.

Brosses, de. *Du culte des dieux fétiches, ou parallèle de l'ancienne religion de l'Egypte avec la religion actuelle de Nigritie*, 1760.

Buschan, G. *Illustrierte Völkerkunde*, Stuttgart, 1923.

Dixon, R.B. *The Building of Cultures*, New York and London, 1928.

Durkheim, E. *De la division du travail social*, 1893.

_______, *Les régies de la méthode sociologique*, 1895.

Ehrenreich, P. *Die allgemeine Mythölogie und ihre ethnologischen Grundlagen,* Leipzig, 1910.

Encyclopaedia of Religion and Ethics, edited by James Hastings, Edinburgh, Vols. I, 1908-XII, 1921. This is an invaluable mine of information, and in it the backward peoples receive adequate mention.

Goldenweiser, A.A. *Early Civilization: an Introduction to Anthropology,* London, 1922.

Gomme, A.B. *The Traditional Games of England, etc.*, London, 1894-98.

Gomme, G.L. *Ethnology in Folk-lore,* London, 1892.

Haddon, A.C. *The Study of Man,* London, 1898.

Hobhouse, L.T., Wheeler, G.C., and Ginsberg, M. *The Material Culture and Social Institutions of the Simpler Peoples,* London, 1930.

Hocart, A.M. *Kingship,* Oxford, 1927.

______, *The Progress of Man: a Short Survey of his Evolution, his Customs, and his Works,* London, 1933.

Jackson, W.J. *Shells as Evidence of the Migrations of Early Culture,* Manchester and London, 1917.

Kraft, Jens. *Die Sitten der Wilden, Zur Aufklärung des Ursprungs der Menschheit* (translated from Danish), Kopenhagen, 1766.

Kroeber, A.L. *Anthropology,* New York and London, 1923.

Lafitau, J.F. *Moeurs des Sauvages comparées aux Moeurs des premiers temps,* 1723.

______, *Histoire des Decouvertes et des conquêtes des Portugais dans le Nouveau Monde*, 1733.

Lang, A. *The Making of Religion,* London, 1898.

______, *Magic and Religion,* London, 1901.

Lippert, J. *Die Kulturgeschichte in einzelnen Hauptstücken,* 1885-86. Translated and edited as *The Evolution of Culture* by G.P. Murdoch, London, 1931.

Lowie, R.H. *Primitive Society,* New York, 1920.

______, *Culture and Ethnology,* 1917.

______, *Primitive Religion,* New York, 1924.

Luschan, F. von. "Zusammenhänge und Konvergenz," *Mitt. d. Anthr. Ges. Wien,* Vol. 48, 1918, pp. 1-117.

Mannhardt, W. *Roggenwolf und Roggehund,* 1865.

______, *Die Korn-dämonen,* 1868.

______, *Der Baumkultus der Gemanen,* 1875.

______, *Antike Wald und Feldkulte,* 1877.

______, *Mythologische Forschungen,* 1884.

Marett, R.R. *Anthropology,* London, 1912.

______, *The Threshold of Religion,* London, 1909.

Meiners, C. (1747-1816). *Grundriss der Geschichte der Menschheit,* Lemgo, 1785.

______, *Untersuchungen über die verschiedenen, Menschennaturen, Tübingen,* 1811.

Perry, W.J. *The Megalithic Culture of Indonesia,* Manchester, 1918.
______, *The Children of the Sun,* London, 1923.
______, *The Origin of Magic and Religion,* London, 1923.
______, *The Growth of Civilization,* London, 1924.
______, *Gods and Men,* London, 1927.
Read, Carveth. *The Origin of Man and of his Superstitions,* Cambridge, 1920.
Rivers, W.H.R. *The History of Melanesian Society,* Cambridge, 1914.
______, *Kinship and Social Organization,* London, 1914.
______, *Instinct and the Unconscious,* Cambridge, 1920; 1922.
______, *Psychology and Politics,* London, 1922.
______, *History and Ethnology,* S.P.C.K., London, 1922.
______, *Psychology and Ethnology,* London, 1926.
Smith, G. Elliot. *The Ancient Egyptians,* London, 1911; 1923.
______, *The Migrations of Early Culture,* Manchester and London, 1915; reprinted in 1930.
______, *The Evolution of the Dragon,* Manchester and London, 1919.
______, *Elephants and Ethnologists*, London, 1924.
______, *In the Beginning,* London, 1928.
______, *Human History,* London, 1930.
______, *The Diffusion of Culture,* London, 1933.
Smith, W. Robertson. *Kinship and Marriage in Early Arabia*, 1885.
Summer, W.G., and Keller, A.G. *The Science of Sociology*, 1927.
Tozer, A.M. *Social Origins and Social Continuities*, 1925.
Tylor, Sir Edward B. *Anthropology,* London, 1881; republished, London, 1930.
Webster, Hutton. *Primitive Secret Societies,* New York, 1908, 1932.
Wissler, Clark. *Man and Culture*, 1923.

Retrospect

On taking a brief final survey of the history of Anthropology, one is struck by the fact that the progress of the science has been very irregular owing to the tendency of students to limit their attention to restricted fields.

Physical anthropology has had very numerous devotees, who have often concerned themselves with small anatomical variations. The criteria of racial anatomy have also been kept in mind, but it is yet uncertain how to describe or to gauge adequately the essential anatomical distinctions between races and peoples. This problem is complicated by our ignorance of the stability of physical characters and of how far or how speedily they are affected by change of environment. It seems desirable that this branch should form part of a wider study, that of Human Biology, which would also embrace the physiological study of man as a living organism, and include human genetics, eugenics, miscegenation, and similar problems. The imperfection of the geological record is answerable for the relatively slow progress that has been made in tracing the evolution of man from his simian ancestors. Ethnology has largely concerned itself with racial classification, but strictly this is a matter for Human Biology.

Whereas the structural characters of man have been studied by trained scientific men, the history of man from a cultural point of view has mainly in the past been investigated by students in museums, and by literary men who have approached the subject from various sides and, from lack of experience in the field or by virtue of their natural reliance upon documentary evidence, have often not been sufficiently critical regarding their authorities. They usually concerned themselves either with comparative studies and theoretical evolutionary processes, or with intensive descriptions of the activities, customs, and beliefs of certain primitive peoples. The study of the latter is a necessary preliminary to the former; though theorists have too often worked on imperfect material, and have frequently made it bear more than it could legitimately carry.

These intensive studies are essential if ever we are to gain a knowledge of the history of mankind; and there is still a very urgent need for their continuance, as the available material is rapidly becoming modified and in many areas is disappearing at an alarming rate.

The fieldworker has to record those conditions which exist and to attempt to recover those which are disappearing or those which have very recently disappeared. In his investigations he will find that, however simple it may at first appear to be, any primitive culture he studies is more or less complex, and in unravelling this complexity he has to determine, as far as he can, the interactions that have taken place and the new conditions or ideas that have arisen therefrom; and it will be found that these new conditions are by no means a simple mixture of two or more ingredients.

The fieldworker has furthermore to extend these historical studies to present conditions, as everywhere there is the problem of the contact with higher civilizations. This newer anthropology requires many thoroughly trained observers, and it is gratifying to find that Colonial Governments are appreciating the fact that, for the wise guidance and control of native races, it is necessary to understand the native point of view, and, as far as possible, to build upon what is best and most stable in native polity. The great difficulty is that the changes in the conditions are too great and too rapid for a more or less orderly evolution to take place, as presumably happened to some extent in the cultural evolution of Europe.

The anthropologist, as such, has merely an informative, or at most an advisory, function, the responsibility for the adjustments between the native culture and the economic requirements of Europeans is the province of the administrator. There is thus a great future of immediate practical utility for anthropologists.

Perhaps the true field of Ethnology should be concerned mainly with: (1) The comparative study of languages and the distributions demonstrated by linguistics. (2) The description of objects made by man (artifacts), their distribution and diffusion in space, and in time (archaeology), their groupings into cultures and the diffusions of these cultures; the relation of Prehistoric Archaeology, or Palaeetlinology, to Ethnology is analogous to that of Palaeontology to Zoology, and the aims and methods of both are those of historical science. (3) The distribution of institutions and religions, a search for their origins; the psychology of individual minds and of groups, and an investigation of the motives which have led individuals to invent and groups to accept particular customs and beliefs. The comparative method has yielded valuable results, but it is liable to lead the unwary into pitfalls. To employ biological terms, analogy is apt to be mistaken for homology, since customs or beliefs (which, it must be remembered, are in the vast majority of cases extremely imperfectly recorded) may have a superficial resemblance, but if all the facts were known, they might be found to have had a very different origin or significance. Comparisons made within a given era or among cognate peoples have a greater value than those drawn from various parts of the world. The comparative method has usually erred in disregarding dissimilarities, which, after all, are as significant as similarities. What is still needed is the intensive study of limited areas, the studies already so made having proved most fruitful.

Although much is known about many forms of social organization, we find that in few cases is the knowledge sufficiently precise to explain them, and there is a lamentable ignorance as to how they function, owing to the fact that the data were not collected by adequately trained observers. If released from the historical-psychological method, Comparative Sociology, as Radcliffe-Brown points out, could concentrate on perfecting its terminology and technique, and thus provide precise descriptions of social and cultural phenomena, and ultimately a systematic classification of those phenomena. A culture is normally an integrated unity in which every element has a distinct function, but the culture as a whole has its own definite mode of functioning; thus whole culture systems should be compared one with another as dynamic rather than as static structures; the French have been the pioneers in this conception of dynamic sociology. It will be more profitable to study the changes that take place in the institutions of a people when some progress has been made in determining what the culture really is and how it works; but it is also true that functional investigations will be greatly helped if a study is made of the changes actually taking place in some aspect of that culture.

Anthropology is slowly becoming a scientific discipline. There are various departments which have been studied separately, but it is being realized that there is a functional nexus that embraces all that man makes, does, and feels, and that it is unscientific to isolate certain activities and to study them as distinct unrelated entities. Being the study of man, it naturally has many points of contact with other departments of knowledge, and it is often difficult to say where one ends and the other begins, but this is more annoying to the librarian than it is to the biologist.

The chief danger to which it has always been liable is that its fascination and popularity, touching as it does every department of human thought and activity, tend to premature generalizations.

In the history of Anthropology, like that of most other sciences, new ideas have often been received with antagonism or neglect, sometimes even before they had been critically examined. This opposition was due to the prejudice and bigotry of those who placed more reliance on tradition or authority than on the results of investigations and the logical deductions therefrom. The danger is still present, but in the past reactionaries always have had to give way in the end, and those views which have stood the test of criticism have ultimately been accepted; and so it will be in the future.

Index

possibility of the transmission of acquired characters. Prichard believed that the transmission of occasional variations might, to some extent, account for the diversities of races. Lawrence wrote more clearly, "Racial differences can be explained only by two principles—namely the occasional production of an offspring with different characters from those of the parents, as a native or congenital variety, and the propagation of such varieties by generation". He considered that domestication favoured the production of these congenital and transmissible variations, and, anticipating the Eugenic school, deplored the fact that, while so much care and attention was paid to the breeding of domestic animals, the breeding of man was left to the vagaries of his own individual fancy.

Sir William Lawrence's (1783-1867) lectures on *Comparative Anatomy, Physiology, Zoology, and the Natural History of Man,* delivered between 1816 and 1818 raised an immediate outcry, and he was charged with the "very unworthy design of propagating opinions detrimental to society, and of endeavouring to enforce them for the purpose of loosening those restraints in which the welfare of mankind depends." He announced publicly that the volumes had been suppressed as he was refused copyright. The *Lectures,* first published in 1819, reached a ninth edition in 1848. Lawrence was far in advance of his time, and much of his teaching may be said to have anticipated the doctrine of evolution. Unfortunately, the theological protest raised by his lectures—published when he was only thirty-five—resulted in his forsaking anthropology altogether.

Another man in advance of his times was Lord Monboddo. James Burnett Monboddo (1714-1799) was regarded as one of the most eccentric characters of the eighteenth century, mainly on account of his peculiar views about the origin of society and of language and his theories as to the relationship of man with monkeys. He not only studied man as one of the animals, but he